With the deepest
of gratitude to the
Okotoks Public Library
for their support of
being the 1st library to
have "Ryken's Journey"
in their book club.

Angel Blessings to those
who read the words I
have written . . .

Love is infinite 💛 Pamela

Ryken's Journey

Pamela Larocque

BALBOA.
PRESS
A DIVISION OF HAY HOUSE

Balboa Press books may be ordered through booksellers or by contacting:

Balboa Press
A Division of Hay House
1663 Liberty Drive
Bloomington, IN 47403
www.balboapress.com
1 (877) 407-4847

Because of the dynamic nature of the Internet, any web addresses or
links contained in this book may have changed since publication and
may no longer be valid. The views expressed in this work are solely those
of the author and do not necessarily reflect the views of the publisher,
and the publisher hereby disclaims any responsibility for them.

The author of this book does not dispense medical advice or prescribe
the use of any technique as a form of treatment for physical, emotional,
or medical problems without the advice of a physician, either directly
or indirectly. The intent of the author is only to offer information
of a general nature to help you in your quest for emotional and
spiritual well-being. In the event you use any of the information in
this book for yourself, which is your constitutional right, the author
and the publisher assume no responsibility for your actions.

Any people depicted in stock imagery provided by Thinkstock are
models, and such images are being used for illustrative purposes only.
Certain stock imagery © Thinkstock.

Cover Design by: Pamela Larocque
Author Photos taken by: Stacey Sharp, Birth Doula

Print information available on the last page.

ISBN: 978-1-5043-5724-1 (sc)
ISBN: 978-1-5043-5726-5 (hc)
ISBN: 978-1-5043-5725-8 (e)

Library of Congress Control Number: 2016907228

Balboa Press rev. date: 07/27/2016

love is

INFINITE...

Ryken's Journey

is a message
to inspire
hope and healing
for those that are
searching for answers
like I was.
The answer that
I found was this...

love is infinite

DEDICATION

This book is dedicated to my children. Without your existence I would not have the privilege to be a mother. It is because of each of you that I aspire everyday to be the best version of me. I love each of you unconditionally, today, tomorrow and always.

To my husband Brett, who had promised to be by my side through the good and bad, during the laughter and the tears, and that nothing could ever change his love for me. My life has been easier to walk along this bumpy road because I was with you. I am filled with the deepest of gratitude and absolute adoration for being the greatest father any child could ever have. Thank you for your unconditional support and love to write this book about our life and encouragement to share "Ryken's Journey" with the world.

To the family and friends that encouraged me along the way. Your kind words gave me the strength to continue on when I needed it the most. To my "unofficial" editors, Stephanie, Stacey and Deanna, who's help was invaluable to me and this book.

To Sally Ann Elliot and Dr. Aaron Chui for the gift of being blessed to have had them in my life as part of our parenting journey and our medical team along the way. It is with the deepest of gratitude to have their written words and names attached to "Ryken's Journey".

To others like me. I have written this book for those of you who will resonate with "Ryken's Journey" and the loss of a baby. May it help you to find your own inner strength to heal so you too can find peace and serenity. This is also for parents of healthy children. May you hug them, love them and feel the deepest gratitude for the wonderful gift that each child is.

To Ryken, my angel son. There are no words to explain the depth of my love for you. Thank you for sending butterflies of encouragement and all the messages to step forward with your book when I wanted to give up. I know that you are always by my side, sending love my way. Until we meet again, I will continue to be the best version of me in honor of you. Sending you many hugs and kisses to heaven. Our love is infinite, boundless and effortless, forever.

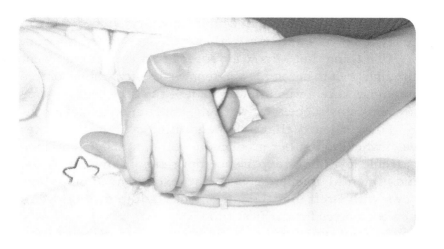

INTRODUCTION

H ave you ever thought your life was going to go in one direction? The path ahead was filled with ignorant bliss. Each step you took brought such joy and wonder that you could not wait to take another turn to see what was around the next bend? But when your whole world collapses, you do not know how to clean up the debris. That is what has happened to me.

I am unsure when the idea came to me that I would write a book about Ryken's life. I had been journaling and writing my entire life to release feelings and emotions that were painful. It is a release for me, and it clears my mind.

After the loss of my baby, I filled wicker baskets with journals. Random thoughts and happy memories filled some pages. The rest of the pages were compiled of the painful memories. I used writing as a tool to release the grip that my grief had around my heart.

I now know, that I have been divinely guided to write this book. I am working hard on listening to the messages that find me. It is amazing what I am hearing now that I am ready to listen. I anticipate other messages on the horizon. One thing that I know for sure is that everything I went through prior to becoming a parent was in preparation for this new adventure. I was unaware of it at the time because they seemed catastrophically agonizing, but I am certain of it now.

I have heard that the pendulum swings the other way; when you suffer great pain, you can also experience extreme joy. I have experienced pure joy in my life. These monumental moments were the exchange of marriage vows with Brett and the gift of looking into my children's newborn faces for the first time.

Without a shadow of a doubt, the responsibility I felt for my babies was beyond anything I had ever experienced before. I was responsible and dependable, but becoming a mother brought those qualities to a much higher level. I had very high expectations of myself as a mother.

When my children were born, I felt unconditional love for them. My helpless babies depended on me for everything, and it felt overwhelming at times. My heart was so full of love for my children; there is nothing I would not do for them.

Before becoming a parent, I thought I knew everything. My eyes were opened wide when my new role happened. I realized I could easily second-guess what I thought I knew about life when it came to my children. I began to learn to trust my own instincts again. People always want to offer advice to new parents. I always did the best I could in each given moment. In becoming a parent, I found a deeper appreciation for my own parents as well. I know that they always did the best they could.

I am ready to share my story because I have a higher purpose. This purpose is to share Ryken's story. Timing is everything; this phrase is used often. I have to agree with it. I was not ready years ago, but I am ready now.

This book is part of my life journey, and it describes my second son's entire life. This is a candid and heart-wrenching account of my baby's life on earth. It is told through my eyes, my heart, and my soul. Ryken's career path was to be a Teacher. I am no different than any other mother who loves her child unconditionally. I want Ryken to fulfill his life purpose and to be able to complete his destiny on earth. For that is what we are each born to do before returning home to the other side.

Without further ado, this is Ryken's journey.

CHAPTER 1

Let's Start at the Beginning

I was born at 8:20 on an autumn morning to parents who could not have been more different. They were like yin and the yang. With my mom and dad, opposites definitely attracted.

When I was born, my nineteen-year-old mother could not believe I was truly hers. She said, "You were the cutest baby on earth. I was in awe that you were truly mine—a beautiful baby to love and cherish."

I asked my dad his thoughts about becoming a father at the age of twenty-one. He said, "You were a little miracle. I had worked all day, and we stayed up all night waiting for you. It was a long night for your mom and me. When you were finally born, your mother was played out—and so was I."

Mothers go through pregnancy and all the changes that occur during that time. We give up many things and focus on eating healthily for the growing baby. We endure the pain during labor. Some women give birth without any medication. We push—for hours sometimes—to get the baby out of our bodies and into the world. And the dad is exhausted? This is an important life lesson. We must not forget how hard it is on the dads when babies are trying to enter the world.

I grew up in a small farming and cattle community as the eldest of three girls. Our parents separated shortly after Christmas when I was eleven. There was no reconciliation, and they eventually divorced. I am very close to my two younger, biological sisters, Deanna and Mindy; they were eight and six when our family changed. I have always had a motherly instinct toward each of them, and it only magnified after the separation. That is the joy of being the firstborn daughter.

I am sure this motherly instinct did not serve any of us well growing up, but that was how it was. My sisters thought I was bossy. I told them it was not easy being the oldest in the family. I guess being bossy was one of my perks. Life really is about our own individual perception.

Growing up, I was the only person I knew who came from a split home. My parents found new partners, and the blended families began. My three new sisters were all younger than me. I was blessed to have the addition of a stepmom, stepdad and sisters in my life; they brought love and many life lessons that helped me grow as a person.

I graduated from high school and was bound and determined to make a life outside of my community. I had dreams about exploring the great big world. I was taking classes for engineering, and university was difficult the first year. When I failed physics and calculus, my hopes of becoming an engineer went up in flames.

My dad told me that summer that I was not quitting university. I would go back and complete a degree of some kind. That was the best advice my dad ever gave me. I returned to my hometown for the summer to work and save all the money I could for my next year of university. The summer months dragged on and I could not wait to return to school that September. My next plan of action was completing my psychology degree.

As summer slowly slipped by and September finally came around, it was during my second year of university, I met my best friend, Jenna. We were enrolled in the same

French class. There is no one like her in the world. She was as beautiful on the inside as she was on the outside. Along with being funny, giving, thoughtful, kind, and loving, I have the privilege to call her my "bestie." I owe it all to a second language.

I set my sights on obtaining a psychology degree. I loved my Psychology 100 class and figuring people out. My first semester went great, and I was enjoying this second year of university. I was over the moon that I had not failed any classes either.

In the middle of my second semester, I struck up a conversation with the cashier at the convenience store by my apartment. I was asking her where she planned to work with her completed psychology degree. She had just graduated and could not find a job in her field. She was working at the store full-time to support herself and pay back her student loans.

I was dumbstruck. I paid for my drink and left whatever plans I had in my mind for completing my psychology degree behind with the cashier at the till. That was divinely orchestrated to help me shift toward a different life path. When one door closes, another one opens. I was looking for an open doorway.

As I walked back to my apartment through the snow, I wondered exactly what I was going to do with my life. I am a realist. I could already work at the convenience store, but the idea of working there after completing four years of university did nothing for me. By this time, I would have incurred a $36,000 student loan that I would be responsible for paying off. There was no passion for me anymore to follow through with a psychology degree. I had no plans to get my master's degree in psychology either so this idea went up in smoke faster than my engineering career dream did.

I realized I had to figure out something else. I was at a loss and was reaching out for help. Fate intervened once more and helped me again. I was guided toward social work, and that is when the pieces of the puzzle started to fall into place for me.

I applied to the social work program at a different university in a different city as well and was accepted. Each year of school became easier; I loved my classes and my teachers. I was beginning to feel like I was born to be a social worker.

I made friends with three amazing women who were also aspiring to complete their degrees in social work. We were the "four musketeers," and I knew our friendship would last a lifetime. We spent a lot of our time together—both in and out of the classroom. We began chatting about backpacking in Europe after graduation.

One of my dreams as a young girl was to travel far and wide. I was interested in France especially. My great-grandmother had lived there, and my maternal grandfather was born there. I always had a strong bond with my great-grandmother. I grew up right across the street from her and would visit her almost daily as a child. She and I would look at her picture albums over cookies in her apartment. We would go into the common area of the building and play shuffleboard together. Sometimes my sisters would be with us, but most of the time, we were by ourselves. I hold those special memories dear to my heart.

While I was at the university, I returned to my hometown during the summer months and worked as a nurses' aid in the health center. My great-grandmother was in her late nineties by then and resided at the center. It was a real gift to be able to help her and care for her during those times.

I graduated from the university with a bachelor of science in social work and a concentration in psychology. I came back home and one month later moved to the city where I had first begun my journey. My new job was working with families that had all kinds of issues and severe addictions. My job was never boring, and it proved to be quite a challenge.

The best part was developing relationships with the families I worked with. It is amazing how you can help people become motivated to make changes within themselves when the relationships are based on respect and trust.

Life was falling into place, and my career was unfolding before my eyes. I was twenty-three years old and working with families that had various issues. I was trying my best to motivate changes in their lives. At the same time, I was working on changing me.

Being a social worker sounds a lot better than actually being one at times. When you meet the families, you become attached to the children and the parents. It is difficult to keep your heart at a distance. I wore my heart on my sleeve for the entire world to see. You could put some of my DNA under a microscope, and it would say "highly sensitive person" in my cellular makeup.

Many of those people still hold special places in my heart. It was a privilege to be a part of their lives, and it was a gift to watch them learn and grow. I was a firsthand witness to seeing families make the necessary changes to make better lives for themselves and their children. It was very inspiring for me as a young social worker to see this.

I had begun my own personal journey of self-healing and was learning a lot about myself during that time. I began counseling to deal with my own issues from the past. I became a "counseling junkie", and I had no shame in it. I began attending Al-Anon meetings weekly to work through my own codependency issues.

I also saw a counselor for years. She was nothing short of a miracle for me. She helped me so much, and I am so grateful for the many hours we shared in her office.

I completed a twelve-step codependency group that changed my life. The gentleman who ran the group was a recovering alcoholic and really helped me realize that it is a disease. I learned compassion along with the gift of setting healthy boundaries for myself.

It is interesting where all of us fall on the spectrum of codependency. If you don't agree with me, then you are still in denial—and that is okay. Sometimes ignorance is bliss. I clearly remember being blissfully ignorant. When I got to my early twenties, I could not pretend anymore. I will always be eternally grateful to the many counselors who helped me along the way.

A wonderful friend at my place of employment took me under her wing and helped me along on my life path. She was my saving grace at the office. Her kindness and the life skills she shared with me to help me become a better and more organized social worker will never be forgotten.

As a Libra, I wake up each morning and say, "Today, I will be organized!" Some days, it works. Fellow Libras will understand when I say, "Some days it won't."

My friend introduced me to an angel card reader. I was raised Catholic and had a strong faith in God. I also had a deep curiosity about this other side of spirituality. During this time I had also been going to many different churches in the city to learn and explore the many sides of religion. I was beginning to learn that I had a "spiritual soul" inside of me. I was twenty-four years old and open to many things.

The card reader was so kind and welcoming. She reminded me of a grandma. In the reading, she said that my next relationship would be very important. I would meet my soul mate. I had recently written a list of what I wanted in my next relationship: I wanted a partner who was confident, smart, funny, kind, romantic, ambitious, accepting, loving, calm, understanding, determined, supportive, and good with kids.

I enjoyed the angel card reading and continued on my life path of working and spending time with family and friends. I was enjoying being single. I didn't think much about the angel reading at the time. I had gone on a few dates, and I had a series of questions. I'd ask, "Are you homophobic?" If my date said, "Yes, I am," that was the one and only date. One of my best friends is gay. There is no one as wonderful or as loyal and kind as her. She has made an incredible difference in this world in regard to ensuring a better life for children. I was not going to have a relationship with anyone who was judgmental about that topic. Some people won't date a smoker, and I won't date anyone who is homophobic. Discussion closed—end of story.

I also refused to settle in a relationship. I refused to waste my time in a relationship that was not going to meet my standards. I had expectations, and they were very cut and dry. I had my list, and I was not swaying from it or compromising.

Instead of worrying unnecessarily about finding a boyfriend, I focused on my own dreams and desires. I was sorting out my own issues through counseling. My goal for dealing with my past issues was very clear. I did not want to bring any of my luggage into my next relationship. I was working on changing my communication pattern to being assertive at all times and with everyone in my life—at work and outside of work. It was a difficult task but not impossible.

I cleaned house internally. It felt amazing. Being alone without a partner and sorting out who I was felt amazing too. Learning how to stand up for my needs and myself was really important and changed my life. The key to self-care and peace is learning how to be assertive and setting boundaries in a kind way. I was also working on what I wanted to do in my life. I had a deep desire to travel and see the world. The key to true happiness is a high level of self-love and a strong sense of self-worth. I was working on it, and I was very happy.

In 1998, the musketeers and I were talking about taking our trip to Europe in the spring of 1999. We tossed around the idea of backpacking for a month and touring different countries. France was on the top of my list due to my childhood visits with my great grandmother.

As the months flew by, Raya and Kali had entered into serious relationships. Dara and I were both single, and we began to plan our adventure abroad. It is amazing how an idea is planted and begins to grow. I was already practicing the art of manifesting, but I did not know it.

Christmas 1998 came and went, and I had no idea there was going to be a special surprise from Santa the following evening. The universe was about to answer my prayers; I just didn't know it yet.

My youngest sister had talked me into going to the Boxing Day Cabaret in the small rivalry town close to where we grew up. That is where I met my future husband.

Like me, Brett had left home right after completing high school to pursue postsecondary education. A few weeks prior to that evening, I had met Brett at a friend's house. I had only dropped in for a few moments. When I met Brett, his eyes attracted my attention. I have read that you know someone by their eyes because souls can recognize another soul this way. It did not surprise me that I was first mesmerized by Brett's eyes.

We found each other by coming home to celebrate the holidays with our families. Life has a way of leading us down the paths we are meant to be on.

The night I met Brett, I put him through the wringer and asked him every question under the sun. Are you homophobic? His answer was no. What does true love mean to you? He said, "Two as one." There were many more questions, and he passed them all with flying colors. We exchanged phone numbers, and Brett called me the following week. We began hanging out and were getting to know each other. Brett worked away for a ten-day period. We would talk on the phone daily when he was gone, and we would spend his four days off together.

We developed a supportive and respectful friendship. We shared the same interests in life. Each of us had the same dreams and desires of traveling and seeking adventures. We genuinely loved to be together and enjoyed each other's company. Being with Brett was easy and fun for me. Each time he had to leave and go back to work was harder for both of us.

During this time, Dara and I were saving our money and planning to fly out on April 28 for our European adventure. We bought our Eurorail passes and picked the countries we would explore together. We had no set agenda, and we were going to see where we would go once we arrived on England's soil.

Then some wonderful news came my way. In March, Raya was getting married. She was the first one to take that leap of faith. I was given the prestigious distinction of being her maid of honor. I really liked her fiancé, Kohen, and he had given me great advice exactly one year before.

He said, "Pam, are you dating Mr. Wrong because you have nothing better to do? What if you are having coffee with Mr. Wrong, and Mr. Right walks into the coffee shop. What happens if you are too busy hanging out with Mr. Wrong? You will miss out on Mr. Right because you are hanging out with Mr. Wrong. And he is not right for you or what you want in life. Am I wrong?" Kohen was definitely right. It was great advice, and I took it. I spent the next ten months by myself. That is when I completed my "must have" partner list along with figuring out who I was and beginning to really love and enjoy the life I was creating for myself.

The important part of this equation was that I was open to listening to Kohen at that time. There have been times in my life when I was not ready to listen—no matter who the people were or what advice they were trying to give me.

I am not the only one who had to learn the hard way. I know that life is about planting seeds with people and releasing the control of when the seeds take root and grow. My soil was dry, and all the nutrients were used up. I was thirsty for the truth and some insight. I was ready to listen when Kohen spoke to me a year ago.

His words shook my world, and that is when my list began. I wrote out my list of what I wanted in a relationship.

I set my inner compass, chose a new path of self-care, and began a new journey. I was on a completely different path and focusing on what I needed and wanted in my life. I chose not to settle because I was needy and lonely. I chose to be the captain of my own ship, and it felt amazing. Realizing that at the age of twenty-four was empowering for me.

I let go of the need to find that person and began trusting that we would find each other. I allowed the universe to be in charge. It was a difficult task for someone like me since I have control issues. I was tired of the life I was leading. Shortly after that, the universe led me to Brett.

At the same time I ended some friendships that I felt were not working for me anymore. I chose to spend time with people who had the same interests. It was nice to be able to find out who I truly was and be true to myself for a change.

Brett and I traveled together to Raya's wedding. It was a beautiful and intimate ceremony tucked away in the mountains. I was very happy for the new couple—and that I had Brett to share the special day with.

After dating for three months, we knew in our hearts that we would spend the rest of our lives together. I had never had those feelings for another human being: strong friendship, unconditional love and support, and absolute adoration for each other. The best thing about our relationship is deep respect and regard for one another. At the core of any intimate relationship, there is a need for a strong friendship.

Life really could not have been any better for me. Actually, it did get better when my trip to Europe arrived!

At the end of April, I was having difficulty choosing what to bring. I only had a backpack. The clothes on my bed would not all fit. I called Kali and asked for help. She came over and helped me out. She was the queen of packing light and prioritizing clothing for a trip like that! Even though she was unable to come with us as planned, she was able to help me pack the night before I left. I am eternally grateful and felt like she was with me on the amazing journey—at least at the beginning of it.

Raya shared with us that she was expecting her first baby. This was the reason she also would not be travelling with us to Europe. So it would still just be two musketeers after all. Dara and I flew to London, took a train to the ferry, and boarded the big boat that crossed over the waters to bring us to France. It was all done in twenty-four hours. We were exhausted by the time we got to our hotel room in France. If I had talked to Brett that first night, I would have flown back home for a nickel to be with him. Thank goodness for sleep. A good solid nine hours of it cured my desire to go home.

The following day we got on the Eurorail to travel to the South of France. Life was grand again, and we were ready for our adventure.

Dara and I hopped on the train and realized that we did not have a reservation at the castle that had been converted to a youth hostel. Our concern was getting there and having nowhere to sleep. I left my backpack with Dara and went to make the call inside the train station to secure a room for us that night.

I stepped off of the train, and my intuition told me to see when the train was going to leave. I walked over to the Eurorail staff member and asked my question in English, hoping he would understand. He motioned for me to board and said, "Direct, direct." I was quite ahead of the car Dara was in, and I jumped on the one that I was standing beside. I understood that the train was about to leave. I started to walk through the cars to the back of the train to find Dara.

I found Dara in the doorway of the train. She was as pale as a ghost. Dara had her backpack on, and she was holding my backpack in front of her. She said, "I thought you were gone. I thought you were in the station on the phone."

I said, "I am so sorry, Dara. We won't separate anymore. If we have to figure out something, we'll get off together." I hugged her and felt awful. Thank God we weren't separated. I can't even imagine what that would have felt like for either of us.

I wished that Raya and Kali were with us. Dara and I were too trusting in life. I am so thankful I followed my intuition and asked the gentleman when the train would leave. I gave Dara another hug. I was glad we learned that valuable lesson within the first few days of our trip. I said a silent prayer that we would make it home safely. I knew it was going to be a life-changing adventure for each of us.

The trip was everything I had hoped for and more. A significant book crossed my path in Italy. In life, we meet many amazing people who help change our destinies. An American backpacker shared her book with me. It was written by Michael Newton and called *Journey of Souls*. It was about case studies of *life between lives*.

I read it in two days, and it resonated deep within me. I knew I was reading what I already knew. We reincarnate so our souls can learn. There are people who are our soul buddies, our soul mates, and part of our soul group. We are born together so we can grow and learn. I was raised Catholic and believed in God, yet this book was fascinating to me.

I had talked to Brett constantly on the phone while I was away, and he had a hefty cell phone bill. Dara and I cried on a boulevard in Paris because we missed our boyfriends so much. Another girlfriend we were traveling with told us to suck it up since those boyfriends would be there when we got home. She said, "We are in Paris for crying out loud!"

She was right. Live in the moment and enjoy it. So we did. Sometimes a kind but firm reality check helps. Living in the moment never felt so true for me.

When I returned home, I was so empowered by what I had seen on my Europe expedition, but it does not take long for the reality of living and working to sink back in again. The summer brought many changes. Brett applied for a job in the city where I lived. We wanted to take the next step in our relationship and live together. Raya and Kohen had a healthy baby boy. They were so happy, and life had changed for them in a positive way. It was hard to believe one of the musketeers had become a mother.

The best part of my everyday life was Brett. I felt like the luckiest girl after meeting him. We had been dating for eight months. Brett got a promotion, and we moved in together on his birthday, August 27. We found a two-bedroom apartment near many walking trails. It was perfect for us, and our new life together began. We were elated that the long-distance relationship was over. A new chapter in our lives was beginning.

At the same time I was not feeling very good physically. I was at my heaviest weight—even though I ate well and exercised daily when I had the energy, and was extremely tired and lethargic.

As a teen, I had been diagnosed with anemia. I had very low iron and was prescribed red iron pills to boost my iron levels. It did not help, and I was prescribed the green iron pills. When that did nothing to raise my iron levels or my energy, my doctor gave me iron shots.

The iron shots were not helping, and I felt awful. I am not one to just sit and wait for help. I began researching the body and other areas that could help me get better. I told myself that somewhere there was someone who could help me.

My good friend from my work recommended someone who helped me immensely. I saw a homeopathic doctor, and my prayers were answered. Dr. Poe asked me many questions. He asked about the water where I lived when I was a teen. My parents had tested the water on our farm, and it came back with the recommendation that it was "fit for infants." However, the water we showered in had changed the ends of our hair to a rusty orange color. There was no need for hair dyes or highlights for my sisters and me. The water had iron in it, and it showed up in our hair. It was not exactly the shade I was looking for.

The naturopathic doctor told me the iron in the water had poisoned my body. The iron supplements I was taking were making it worse and were continuing to poison me. I could not agree more. I felt worse than I did before all of the iron supplements and iron shots.

He prescribed me a white iron homeopathic remedy that cost me six dollars. I took drops under my tongue a few times daily for the next few weeks. I watched the iron start to leave my body. It was the beginning of my road to a healthier me.

I went for healing sessions with a well-known mother-and-daughter team in a town close to where I grew up. They combined reflexology with energy work, and body alignment. They had true healing gifts from God. They prescribed homeopathic medicines and B12 shots for me. I also used iodine on my feet for my thyroid, and they aligned my body properly.

At my first treatment, they told me that my body would not be able to carry a baby. I was not ready to become a mother yet, but Brett and I wanted children someday. It was concerning, and I committed to seeing them regularly. I was driven to be healthy and feel better.

Six months later, I realized how good I was feeling. It is funny how you do not realize how terrible you feel until you begin to start feeling good again. I was getting in touch with my physical body on a much deeper level. My health was on an upward swing, and I was thoroughly enjoying life.

On the morning of February 17, 2000, my mom called me at work. Through her tears, she told me that my Grandma Isabelle had passed away that morning. My grandparents were on a vacation, and my grandfather was trying to deal with the death of his beloved wife.

I cried at my desk as I listened to the words. My grandma's heart had stopped as they were having coffee in their hotel room that morning. She was gone at the age of sixty-six. There was no one in the world like my beautiful grandma. She was so kind and loving and was the sweetest woman I knew. I was very close to her, and I adored her with all of my heart. She was my favorite person, and a piece of my heart broke that day.

Grandma Isabelle was the first person I lost who I really felt should have lived longer. She was also the first person I lost where I really felt overcome by my loss. I went through the stages of grief. I tried to cope and continued on with my everyday life. I had a few counseling sessions to help me deal with my loss. Talking and acknowledging my feelings in a safe environment has always been key for me.

I had no regrets since I had always spent a lot of time with her. I had told my grandma how special she was to me when she was alive. I was not shy about telling her that I loved her and just how special she was to me. I felt that I had left no stone unturned, which helped me through my grief.

I felt a deep sadness for my grandfather as well. He was ten years older than Grandma and missed her terribly. The silver lining of grandma's death at such an early age was that our grandfather became closer with his children and their families. He had said there was no one like her, and he was right. She was a true blessing to our family.

As life continued, I was able to pass a graveyard without bursting into tears about my grandma. That was a step toward acceptance.

Death has a way of making me evaluate my own life. I wanted to be healthier—and stay healthy when I am a grandma later on in life. When I returned home, I was so empowered by what I had seen on my trip. I realized I needed to further my physical healing journey, and my next step was having colonics. My wonderful massage therapist had shared the health benefits of colonics and was also trained in giving them.

According to medicinenet.com, a colonic is "the infusion of liquid into the colon through a tube in the rectum." I would have to agree with this definition. I had five colonics in a fourteen-day span to cleanse my colon. I also took a high-quality probiotic each day to put the good bacteria back into the colon that had been washed away during the flood.

I was very happy with the results, and I had truly never felt better. Don't knock it until you try it. I really noticed my health improving after the intervention, and I am very thankful I did it. The coating on the iron pills I had taken for all those years had left a mark on my colon. The colonics got rid of the coating from the pills that was stuck to my intestinal walls.

I realized how sick I had been before I started my healing journey. I am curious about how I was able to complete my university degree, maintain a full-time position as a social worker, or hike in Europe when I was not feeling well. Maybe it was mind over matter. Adrenaline can help our bodies do things that are difficult.

When we decide to do something, it is amazing what can happen. Our bodies are amazing. I set out with the intention to heal as best as I could. I was on a path to a healthier me, and the people I was meeting along the way were helping me immensely.

For a year and a half, life moved along joyfully and effortlessly for Brett and I. Life was pleasant, calm, and peaceful. I was the happiest I had ever been. I loved my job, and Brett returned to university to complete his engineering degree.

We saved our money and went to an adults-only resort in Cuba for his February break. We planned to enjoy a week of relaxation and fun. The sand was crystal white, and the color of the water was stunning. Our resort was everything the travel agent had said it would be.

Brett proposed to me on our second night there. It was as romantic as you can imagine. He got down on one knee, placed a beautiful trinity ring on my finger, and asked me to marry him. I said yes and pulled him up for a kiss. We left the beach arm in arm and searched for a place to commemorate our memorable event.

We went to the piano lounge to have some champagne and heard "Imagine" by John Lennon. During the early phase of our relationship, Brett and I had agreed that it was the best song ever written. I felt like the stars had aligned for us. I could tell the universe was telling us that we were meant to be together. I already knew it, but the validation from the universe was nice. Nothing in this life is coincidental—at least it's not in mine.

We returned home and told everyone the wonderful news. We decided to get married on July 27, 2002. Brett and I had shared our first kiss on December 27, 1998. We moved in together on August 27, 1999. The number twenty-seven is very significant in our relationship and so July 27th felt right for our wedding date. Life continues on and I love being engaged to Brett.

For Labor Day, my sisters and I went to visit some of our favorite cousins for a girl's weekend. We returned home on the Monday evening, which was a holiday. I had missed Brett and could not wait to see him. My sisters and I entered our apartment together, and Brett had a look on his face. I hugged him, and Brett spoke words that would forever change the world, as I knew it. "Pam, Raya called. Kohen has died. She called here earlier today and said he drowned at the family reunion at her mom's place." I could not believe it and began to cry. My sweet Raya. I had flashbacks of Kohen. The first time I met Kohen, he had picked me up from the airport because Raya was working. He had a sign with my name on it.

We hit it off right away, and he was like a big brother to me. I spent almost a week with them. I was able to see how wonderful Kohen was to Raya, and it made me happy. Their relationship showed me what life could be like with someone who is healthy, kind, and loving. I will never forget my time with them or what I learned from them about myself.

Kohen made me look at myself and realize what I really wanted in life. I remembered their wedding and the love they shared. My favorite thing about him was how much he truly loved my friend. He took such good care of Raya and their son.

I cried for Raya. One of my best friends was now a young widow. She had lost her husband after only having a short life together. I said good-bye to my sisters as they left to go home and called Raya. She picked up after the third ring and relayed to me what had happened through her tears. I could hear the numbness and shock in her voice. I listened to the tragic news and felt helpless.

Kohen was not a great swimmer, and there was a drop-off on the bottom of the man-made lake. There was also an undercurrent in the lake. Raya was at her mother's house up the road with their son when it happened. Many other family members were swimming as well. Everyone was affected by his drowning. I could not understand how the world could be so cruel. It is hard to imagine it was his time to go. Kohen was amazing and loved by everyone.

I got off the phone and hugged Brett. The tragedy taught me that you never know when someone you love will be gone. A person should work on living with gratitude for the people in their life each and every day.

The other musketeers and I rallied together and flew out to be with Raya for the funeral. It was awful to watch someone we loved suffer and grieve. There was nothing we can do to alleviate her pain except to be there for her.

Raya was so strong and always put her son's needs first. She was such a good mother to her child. I am so thankful that she has a supportive family who she can rely on to help her through her loss. Many people do not have the support they need when they are grieving. Life continues after someone has died. For us, it was no different. We had to get back to our own lives and leave Raya knowing she would never be the same.

Raya and I spoke regularly. She worked on taking care of herself and her son. I was so proud of her. I could not imagine my life without Brett. I loved him beyond words and wanted to be with him forever.

Every day, Raya had to wake up and face a world that did not have her husband in it. She was raising their child on her own, and I have the greatest admiration for her strength and courage.

The following year, we flew out for the one year anniversary of Kohen's death. We traveled with Raya and her young son to the place where they had lost him. We listened to Raya and cried with her. There was anger, sadness, laughter, and love. Over many hugs and tears, we shared stories and memories about Kohen.

We did not try to fix Raya's grief. We did not tell her to move on. We were present, kind, and supportive. Raya made sure the weekend was about celebrating Kohen's life and honoring her grief.

I was able to see that support is essential for anyone who is trying to recover from a loss. No matter what you are feeling on your grief journey, you are still loved and cared for—no matter how much time has passed. I believe it was helpful for Raya. The weekend went by too fast as it always does when the musketeers are together.

When we went back to our lives, it was comforting to know that Raya knew we would always be there for her. Even if it could only be a phone call, it was still something. She was managing her life well and had an adorable son who was growing up fast. She would be giving the "toast to the bride" at our wedding in July. That was the next time the musketeers would be together again.

As work and wedding planning continued, the time passed quickly. We had a beautiful ceremony in a United Church with an amazing reverend. Brett was raised United, and my belief system resonated with the religion as well.

The words "two as one" were inscribed in our wedding bands. Brett shared those words with me on the night of our first kiss when I asked him what true love meant to him.

We wrote our own vows separately and exchanged those words in front of more than three hundred family members and friends at two o'clock on the afternoon of July 27. I had an astrologer friend help me pick out the best time to be married. I wanted to ensure that our lives continued to be the best they could be. I took great care in planning our marriage—right down to the tiniest detail. I was a child of divorce, and I took getting married very seriously.

Due to the many parents and stepparents, we decided that Brett's parents would walk down the aisle together first. My dad and stepmother would follow after Brett's parents and then my mom and stepdad. Everyone was acknowledged as a parent. I did not have the uneasiness of walking down the aisle with my mom and dad. I also felt it was a good way of not hurting anyone's feelings. It's amazing how weddings make us want to please others. Thank goodness I had taken that codependency course and dealt with some of my issues a few years ago.

Brett and I are both very independent people. A good friend suggested walking down the aisle on my own. It made sense to me. Brett's two brothers were the groomsmen, and my sisters were the bridesmaids. Brett was waiting to meet me in the middle of the aisle. As I walked toward him that day, I knew my life with Brett would be wonderful. As I stepped closer, he reached out to take my hand. He smiled that smile I fell in love with. As our hands joined and we walked the rest of the way together to commit ourselves to one another, I felt a sense of peace wash over me.

Our beautiful ceremony exceeded all of my expectations. The musicians played "Canon in D," and our new lives began as we exchanged our vows:

Brett, today, I commit my heart to you as your wife. Your love has taught me the meaning of trust and unconditional love. Today, I commit my heart to you as your friend. You are the person I want to walk beside as I journey through life. Today, I commit my heart to you as your soul mate; our love has made my life complete. Today I commit to you and God that I will respect, honor, and cherish you all the days of my life. Two as one, from this day forward.

Pamela, today, I take you to be my wife. You are more than just my wife; you are my partner, my best friend, my one true love, and my soul mate. From the moment we met, I knew there was something special—and I wanted to spend the rest of my life by your side, hearing your thoughts and sharing our dreams. I will be by your side through the good and the bad. During the laughter and the tears. Nothing can ever change my love for you. I promise to love, comfort, and always be there for you, when you need me, as long as we both shall live.

My favorite part of the day was sharing our vows with each other, our guests, and God. I was trembling inside, but Brett softly rubbed my hands with his thumb. It was the best moment of my life up to that point. I was so excited and full of gratitude to be blessed with the privilege of becoming Brett's wife. I felt complete and knew life was the way it was supposed to be.

Following an intimate dinner with our siblings, their partners, parents, and grandparents in a quaint restaurant, we had a reception and dance with more than 350 guests. At midnight, we had the DJ play "Happy Birthday" to my favorite cousin, Garret, who was just turning twenty-seven.

We danced, visited, and left the fun shortly after midnight to make our own fun in the honeymoon suite.

I carried peace and serenity within me during the transition into official married life. Marriage was pure bliss for me. Happiness permeated every cell in my body, and I was in a state of wonder.

We had an amazing honeymoon, which I highly recommend every married couple take right after their wedding. It was a time to treasure each other and the commitment that we made as husband and wife.

On the first day of our honeymoon, we went shopping for folic acid supplements. We were very excited to begin the next phase in our life: parenthood. We strolled barefoot in the sand and talked about getting pregnant and everything that comes with the unknown of becoming parents. I had not thought about having children until I met Brett. It was exciting to think about what our baby would look like. We wondered if we would have a boy or a girl and what the child's personality would be like. I mentioned Brett being in the delivery room and holding my hand.

Brett said, "I don't know if I am going in the delivery room, Pam."

I stopped and looked at him. "You are joking, right?"

"No, I am not. That freaks me out."

"Brett, if I am carrying the baby for nine months, you can be in the delivery room for the birth. Giving birth freaks me out."

"You can't make me go in the delivery room."

I thought back to the list I'd written before we met. I was sure I did not list *stubborn* on it, but maybe I wrote *determined*.

I said, "We better stop talking about this right now—or we will be having our first fight as a married couple on our honeymoon."

Brett made no further comment but he had a *determined* look on his handsome face. Our honeymoon was amazing and remains one of the best memories of my life.

CHAPTER 2

PPP ... Planning, Pregnancy, Parenthood

We returned to the routine of work, the fun of being newlyweds, and the excitement of our plans to start our family. We decided to build a house. We took the plunge into a mortgage, building a new home, and having a family all at once. It was fun and exciting to choose the colors for the walls, the cupboards, the flooring, and everything else that comes with building a house.

It was also fun trying to get pregnant. We were not pregnant instantly, which was disappointing. I thought I'd get pregnant in the first month. I started to track my cycle and was able to determine when I ovulated. I was following the theory of every twenty-eight days. I found out that I ovulate earlier. That first month, I had missed the ideal time to get pregnant. When I was a few days late the following month, I bought a home pregnancy test, which showed that I was not pregnant. I had no period, but I was not pregnant—at least that is what the test said.

October 24, 2002 - journal entry

> *Today Brett and I went to the walk-in clinic
> for a pregnancy test. The results were that I*

was not pregnant. The doctor said if I didn't have my period in two weeks to come back for another test. I talked with a coworker, and she said a friend of hers was negative on the urine test but was positive when the blood test was taken. I decided to wait and try to be patient. I know it's in God's hands. I will continue to live my life and not be consumed with a baby. I need to trust in God. I need to let go since I have no power really—it's all been decided before. I might as well enjoy life and sex for now. Live for today.

So I tried having patience and letting go for the next few days, which is difficult for me. Luckily I have work and Brett to distract me. Finally, after one long week of being late, we went back to the doctor for another urine test. The nurse came back and confirmed that I was indeed pregnant! Due date: July 2, 2003! It was one of those life-changing moments where I felt like I was floating on air.

November 21, 2002 – journal entry

We found out we were pregnant on November 2. It was exciting for us. We went to Planned Parenthood, and the same nurse who was at the walk-in clinic ten days earlier gave us the test. That was quite interesting. It was nice to see a familiar face.

We went to our family doctor on November 18, and she confirmed that we were seven weeks and two days pregnant. She ordered blood tests and a urine test. She said the due date would be July 5. The nurse from the clinic had predicted July 4. Regardless it's a summer baby—right before our one-year anniversary.

*I had morning sickness for two days
(November 13 and 14). I have been extremely
tired and moody. My emotions are raw, and
I felt as though I'm walking through life in
a daze. I cry over small things. I'm quite
nervous and worried and scared all at once.*

*My next doctor's appointment is with the ob-
gyn on December 17 at noon. We might be
able to hear the baby's heartbeat. I am going
to try to rest now. Bye for now baby.*

That following weekend, we went home for a big, extended family reunion and an early Christmas celebration at my parents' home. I was so excited to share our news. We knew couples that had been trying to have babies but were still not pregnant. I was mindful enough to know that sharing our joy about our baby with them could possibly hurt their feelings. It could be an uncomfortable topic for some.

I handed my mom her Christmas card and waited with joy in my heart. She opened it and read the words about becoming a grandma.

Christmas Poem 2002

*Christmas brings many blessings, both big
and small. Some are expected, and some
you'd never guess at all. It's an exciting
year for the newly married couple because
on the American holiday of Independence
Day, a new bundle of joy is expected their
way. A healthy baby boy or girl, completely
innocent, will enter their world, so get used to
the name of Grandma and Grandpa because
that's what you'll be in July 2003. There'll be
no more nagging and begging, wishing and*

> *hoping, crying and complaining. Our dream*
> *has come true; we're having a baby!*

Once we were married, everyone was asking, "When are you having a baby?"

Life is funny sometimes. Luckily for us, we wanted a family of our own. Some people never want to have kids and still get asked that question. When they say never, the looks they get from people must drive them nuts. We could not wait though to become parents.

We were able to share the news with our families that Christmas since we were just past the twelve-week mark. I still have pictures of their faces and their tears of happiness. Brett's Mom was so excited too! I have pictures to show our firstborn how crazy the grandparents were. The grandparents were smiling from ear to ear. Our baby would be the first on either side to hold and snuggle.

My mom quit smoking one week after hearing she would be a grandmother. She wanted to get healthy for her first grandchild. It's amazing what the news of a grandbaby can do!

Thus began our adventure into parenthood. Brett was finishing his last year of school to complete his engineering degree. We were diving headfirst into building a home, and we were going to be parents. Parenthood was going to be so exciting. It should all be a piece of cake right? We were walking on cloud nine. Life could not have been more wonderful or complete for us.

Something I had always wanted to do finally became a reality for me. When I was five months pregnant, I joined a belly dancing class and loved it. I recommend it for anyone who is pregnant! I really got in touch with my body, and it was fun to do with my baby belly. It was a good workout and did not put too much pressure on my body or joints. I loved it and loved doing it while I was pregnant. It was empowering for me as my body changed each month of the pregnancy, and I got more in touch with myself. I truly embraced the life growing inside of me, and I will always cherish the experience.

My pregnancy continued to go well. My one complaint was the fluid retention. I had gained forty-two pounds by the end of my last trimester. I certainly was feeling uncomfortable.

My full-time job as a social worker was tiring. I was looking forward to my peaceful year with my new bundle of joy. I read *What to Expect When You Are Expecting* from front to back. I took a vegetarian multivitamin that had no iron in it. I had a great doctor who listened and supported my choices. There is nothing in the world like a doctor who takes the time to acknowledge a patient's concerns. I had refused to put any iron into my body, regardless if I was pregnant. Our family doctor was the best.

We moved into our new home in February. If you can move while you are pregnant, do it! Everyone helped us, and I did not have to lift any boxes. It was great!

A wonderful friend I had grown up with helped me by sewing the bedding for our baby's room. We chose a "blue jean teddy bear" theme. It was so adorable! I was able to get a crib mobile with four matching teddy bears. Everything matched—from the bedding to the crib sheets to the blue jean teddy on the wall. The theme would work if our new bundle of joy were a boy or a girl.

I kept walking daily and continued going to the gym for cardio and weightlifting a few times per week. I ate well and had a few chocolate milk shakes that I insisted were baby cravings. At least that was what I told myself whenever I had one in my hand.

We attended our prenatal classes and were entertained through them all by the trainer. Sheila was simply amazing. She was a legend in the prenatal and postnatal baby world where we live. One of my favorite memories of her was during a prenatal class when she was talking about the "burning ring of fire." Sheila put a special neck warmer on her head and described how the baby's head comes out of the mother. She proceeded to demonstrate just how the head would come out and go back in and come out and go back in. She explained how it could last a very long time. We were all laughing, especially the dads.

I was a bit fearful after that session. I was concerned what my own *burning ring of fire* would entail when this little person decided to enter our world.

Next on the to-do list was writing out a birth plan. We discussed it in our prenatal classes. With a birth plan, the new parents shared exactly how they wanted their babies' births to go. We were no different.

Brett agreed to come into the room to be at my side during labor, which made me very happy. The twenty-first century was different than the 1950s when fathers did not go into the delivery room. I guess I married an old soul. I was beyond thrilled that he decided on his own to join his baby and me at the blessed event.

Our Birth Plan

1. *Mother will give birth naturally.*
2. *Decline any pain medication.*
3. *Mother will not have an epidural.*
4. *Father does not want to cut the cord.*
5. *Father does not want to see any of the birth or the baby's head coming out.*
6. *There will be no videotaping of the birth.*
7. *Please place baby on the mother right away.*
8. *Mother would like to nurse right away.*

First-time parents are so naive. They think they have it all figured out. We sure did. As I thought about parenthood, many things crossed my mind. I was curious about what our child would look like. I believed that parenting was going to be easy. We would raise the child to be a happy, productive person in the community. He or she would contribute positively to society. The child would learn

French and go to a French immersion school. Our baby would speak English and French, which would open up the possibility of employment with the federal government.

I would use logical consequences and natural consequences for parenting. It was all black and white in my mind. Parenting was going to be as easy as adding a gate to the white picket fence that surrounded our home, which was already perfect. I had been doing therapeutic counseling with families for six years. Even though I had never been a parent, I had been telling parents how to parent for a long time. I had no concerns about becoming a mother.

It sure is easy to talk about something that I really had no experience in. This parenting thing was going to be easy. Wow. Being naive is such a great way to live.

CHAPTER 3

The Sun Is about to Rise

I worked until the beginning of June, which was a month before my due date. I did some final unpacking and nesting activities before my new bundle of joy would arrive. I had not been sleeping well at night, and I was very thankful for our new green rocker recliner! I could not wait to snuggle our baby as we rocked in it. I was using it for the uncomfortable, sleepless nights I was having already.

We decided we were not going to find out the sex of the baby. We were still working on names. I had picked out my girl name when I was eighteen. Brett loved it as well. If we had a girl, she would be named Cassea. We would call her Cass for short. Her middle name was after Grandma Isabelle. So she would be Cassea Isabelle Larocque. I loved this name!

If our baby was a boy, we agreed on Tristan. Thanks to Brad Pitt's starring role in *Legends of the Fall*, I loved the name. When I was eight months pregnant, I looked up the meaning of it. It meant *sad* in French. I was so disappointed since I really liked that name.

We were so happy and excited about our little bundle of joy. I did not want to have our baby's name represent *sadness*. Regardless of my love for it, it was taken off of

Ryken's Journey

the list. Since we had no boy's name picked out, I was 99 percent positive we would have a boy.

We watched a movie with a character named Aden. I loved the name. Brett said, "No way." We went through the alphabet and rhymed letters with it: Aden, Baden, Caden, Haden, Jaden, Kaden. Hey, that sounds good. I googled *Kaden*. It meant *friend* in Arabic. I almost jumped out of my chair after reading it. I was so excited.

Brett could not find anything to rhyme with the name Kaden. He thought it could be a "bully-proof" name. If Brett could make fun of a name, it was off the list. Dads don't want their kids bullied on the playground because of their names. "A Boy named Sue" by Johnny Cash is a prime example of what we did not want to do to our son.

I placed my hand on my tummy and asked, "Kaden sounds good to me; what do you think?" I felt my baby kick in response, but I was unsure if it meant yes or no. The hard part was over because Brett actually loved the name too.

We also decided to use Brett's middle name: Anthony. Anthony means "priceless," and the smartest, cutest, and most amazing boy name had been decided. Kaden Anthony was chosen with weeks to spare even. Check. I was so happy to have a boy's name and a girl's name for our baby. Life was back to being perfect.

On June 29, Brett went to his brother's house. I was having a lazy Sunday morning in bed since I had not slept so great the night before. I was reading my book and rolled over to get more comfortable. All of a sudden, a huge gush of water poured out of me! My water had broken and continued to break. I was leaking everywhere.

I was smiling like a crazy woman as I got myself out of my bed and grabbed some towels from the closet. I stripped the sheets and thought; *my baby will be here soon*. I could hardly believe it was happening. It seemed like my pregnancy lasted a long time, and within minutes, the time had come.

I called Brett with the news. He left right away and would be home within twenty minutes. All I could think was our baby would be born that day. I couldn't stop smiling and talking to my belly.

I was in a state of excitement. Though I had hardly slept last night, I knew it was the best sleep I would have for months possibly.

Brett came home, and we had some lunch. There were no contractions yet, and I was feeling great. We had been told to go to the hospital when your water breaks—even if there are no contractions. I showered since I felt we had lots of time. We went to the hospital with my overnight bag.

We knew the next time we would be together in the car; there would be a new bundle of joy with us. We were trying to guess if it was a boy or girl. It was fun not to know the sex of the baby. I was admitted to labor and delivery, and my doctor was actually working that day. She would deliver our baby, which was a miracle since they typically each have one day per week on the unit. She explained the protocol and our options. I could go home and wait for the contractions to begin. If the baby is not born twenty-four hours after my water broke, the baby would be admitted to the neonatal intensive care unit.

I could stay in labor and delivery and be induced. I would have my own doctor until seven o'clock the following morning.

It was an easy choice for us. Being naïve is not always a bad thing. I was thinking that the option of being induced couldn't be that bad. We decided on the induction. We called our parents and notified them that the birthing process had begun.

I was hooked up intravenously to the medication. Since I had not started contracting, my medicine was upped. We also began walking the hall with my drip bag of oxytocin. The fun began around six thirty.

My mom and Brett's parents arrived within minutes. The five of us walked and chatted. I would periodically have to stop for a painful contraction. I tried to breathe through them and maintain some poise and self-control.

Every hour, they increased the drip. By eleven o'clock, I could barely walk. The contractions were so painful and were coming every five minutes.

We went back into the delivery room, and I told Brett that he had to tell his parents to go. I told my mom through my tears that she had to leave as well. I could not handle an audience anymore. We would call them shortly to tell them the good news. I was confident the baby would be born within the hour. The pain was so intense.

They left, and I felt better without the parade of excited grandparents. So much excitement surrounded the arrival of our baby. She or he would be the first new grandbaby for everyone to see, feel, and touch. I was in a lot of pain and needed space.

The nurse checked me and I was only four or five centimeters dilated.

I said to her, "How much longer can this go on? Could it last another eight hours?" I could hear the terror in my voice.

She looked me in the eye and said, "Oh, yes. It will last another eight hours for sure. It's your first baby."

I looked at Brett and started to cry. I could not stand another hour of pain—let alone eight more hours. I sat on a bouncy ball to help ease the pain. It did nothing for my pain, but it made the contraction a hundred times worse. I would not be using the bouncy ball for any more contractions! It heightened the pain of the contractions and made me crazier. I would have loved to shove it somewhere, anywhere, but I was through riding out the contractions . with the help of the exercise ball, thank you very much. Here's a tip; stay away from exercise balls after being induced.

I looked into Brett's eyes and said, "I cannot handle another eight hours of this! I need an epidural!" I began to cry. The pain was so intense, and I was having trouble getting through them. I was so disappointed it would not be a natural birth, but I could not stand it anymore. I had heard that the labor pains were worse with an induction. I like to think that I have a high pain tolerance, but I could take no more.

Brett told me that I needed to do whatever I thought was best for me. I had gone into my labor with open eyes and a birth plan. When it's your first time giving birth, you don't know what to expect. I was really clueless.

Babies don't care about birth plans. Being induced was not in the birth plan! I was a bit frustrated to say the least. My nurse went to see what she could do. The anesthesiologist was called and administered the epidural just after midnight. At two o'clock, I was able to sleep for a few hours. I am in favor of epidurals now. It will be the first sentence on my next birth plan..."give mother an epidural as soon as possible". Live and learn is the phrase that comes to mind at this moment in time for me.

When things really started to progress during the last stage of labor, Brett held my left leg. The labor and delivery unit was short-staffed and needed help. I needed help, and Brett saw everything! We could cross that off the birth plan as well. Dad was exposed to everything, even though he did not want to see anything. I had wanted the birth videoed, but Brett had refused. I guess his soul knew his hands would be tied up with my leg!

I was finally ten centimeters dilated, and the baby's head was coming out. Burning ring of fire was the best way to describe it. I heard Sheila's voice in my head. Even with the epidural, it was painful. My doctor had to use the vacuum on the baby since the head was stuck. The baby would not come out. I pushed, as my doctor held tightly to the vacuum and pulled. I prayed my baby would be okay.

I also prayed that the baby would finally come out, and my prayers were answered.

CHAPTER 4

You are my Sunshine

You are my sunshine,
My only sunshine.
You make me happy when skies are gray.
You never know, dear, how much I love you.

At 6:55 a.m. on June 30, 2003, our firstborn finally entered the world. The baby was placed on my chest. It was a boy! Brett was able to opt out of cutting the cord. Finally something was going right on our birth plan!

Kaden Anthony Larocque was welcomed into the world. Brett and I fell in love with our beautiful son instantaneously. Our new baby boy had silky, dark hair and striking brown eyes. We were in awe. He had the most amazing birthmark on the right side of his face, just along his jaw line. I thought, *No one would be able to steal my baby because of his beautiful birthmark!* The weird ideas we get from watching television or reading books.

The nurse asked, "What is his name?"

I proudly replied, "We are calling him Kaden Anthony!" Knowing the name Kaden is so unique and special; I was smiling from ear to ear with pride.

The nurse replied, "I like that name. That is the third Kaden I have delivered in the past four months." What? Our egos were deflated as flat as pancakes. Oh well, we did not care. That was his name, and we were thrilled with him.

Anthony means "worthy of praise" or "highly praiseworthy." In Basque, it means "priceless." Our beautiful baby was destined to be "a friend who was priceless."

I nursed him right away and could hardly believe he had finally arrived. He weighed seven pounds and fifteen ounces. Brett and I bonded immediately with Kaden. It truly was a surreal experience. We called our families with the wonderful news. My mom was at the hospital at eight o'clock to meet her first grandchild.

After nursing him, I gave Kaden to Brett. They went with the nurse for Kaden's first bath. He would also be getting special drops in his eyes.

I went for my own bath, which was heavenly. It is very different to have a bath without a baby in my tummy. It was like whatever had invaded my body had left, but it did not leave my body the same. I placed my hand on my stomach, missing the feel of my pregnant tummy for a brief moment. I had lost twenty-four pounds after giving birth since I had retained so much water during the pregnancy.

All I could think about was that I had a newborn baby boy to hold and take care of. I closed my eyes and rested in the warmth of the water. I basked in the heat and silence. I was trying to come to terms with the fact that a vacuum had helped free my baby from the birth canal. Delivering the placenta was not exactly fun either. To put it mildly, I was relieved it was all over.

I shuddered in the water. The water was still hot, but my body had a mind of its own. I still had the chills and couldn't warm up. I was shaking and shivering in the hot water.

The pleasure of seeing and holding your baby takes away some of the memory of the pain endured to get this special treasure. Our DNA had intertwined to create our little being. I closed my eyes and took a few deep breaths. I washed up and headed out to see my little man.

It was strange knowing my baby was finally here and waiting in the next room for me. After all the months of not knowing what we would be having but instinctively feeling I was carrying a boy, there he was. I had a son to take care of. I could not wait to hold my baby again and look at his sweet face. I had forgot to count his ten little fingers and toes.

I went back to my room in labor and delivery. Brett's dad and brother were in the delivery room with my mom waiting to meet Kaden. The nurse came in and asked them to leave. She told them they could visit when I was released to my room in the mother and baby unit. I had requested a private room. Brett was still going to university, but he was planning to stay with us at the hospital as much as he could. If he stayed overnight, it would be helpful to have some privacy.

Kaden and I were moved within an hour. Visitors surrounded us, and the excitement was so thick I could taste it. He was so loved and adored already.

Kaden ended up having jaundice and had to be placed under the lights in my room. It was so heartbreaking. I could only hold him to nurse; otherwise, he had to have his little shades on and remain in his bassinet to soak up the rays. Brett could not hold him at all, but he offered to change his diapers when needed, which was helpful.

As first-time parents, we were devastated. We sat beside the bassinet and watched Kaden like hawks. We made sure he was breathing and resting. We were so crushed. We already worried about him and how the time alone would affect him. As a social worker, I knew the importance of bonding with a baby.

We held his little finger and never wanted to leave his side. We talked to him and stroked his little body. I had read many books about the importance of holding a new baby. Physical contact was very important. I worried about Kaden having an "attachment disorder." Sometimes ignorance is bliss—and means less worrying for a new mother—but being educated about things can be a double-edged sword.

Our family doctor came and saw Kaden every day—even on her weekend off. On Sunday morning, she asked permission to allow her children to see the "yellow" baby. They were on their way to a family outing, and she wanted to stop at the hospital to check on him. We agreed, and her kids got to see what a jaundiced baby looked like.

She went above and beyond the call of duty as our doctor. She was another earth angel who took great care of my family and our newest addition. I will be eternally grateful for her kindness and amazing bedside manner.

We were there for five days and missed the annual family reunion on my mom's side of the family. I had hoped to show Kaden off to everyone. We were also celebrating my grandfather's eightieth birthday. Priorities change when you are focusing on your new baby.

I had been allowed to stay at the hospital since I was exclusively nursing. I could go home—but not with my baby. I was grateful that my doctor allowed me to remain with Kaden. Brett went home each night and came back to the hospital when he was not in classes.

Nursing was not going well unless you call bleeding and blistered nipples "going well." After a few days, I decided to contact the La Leche League for instructions. I was concerned about my nipples. With lack of sleep and the pain that went with nursing, I was beginning to feel overwhelmed.

A wonderful member and mother who had "previous nursing experience" came to my room and helped me position Kaden. She showed me different holds and gave me some wonderful tips. I highly recommend seeking out a La Leche League in your community during your pregnancy and attending a few meetings. They offer support groups before and after the baby is born and can help if nursing is what you want to do. I wish I had called someone on the day my baby was born. At least I can pass on the information to others.

Ten days after Kaden's birth, the doctors decided he could go home. We were so excited. I felt like Dorothy in *The Wizard of Oz*. The words that were ringing in my head were, "there is no place like home". I was finally going home with my baby in tow.

CHAPTER 5

PPD ... Seriously

I was so happy to be leaving the hospital with our new baby. Those ten days in the hospital were the longest of my life! Even though we changed Kaden's diaper and stroked his skin, it was not the same as holding him in our arms.

I wanted to get home and begin motherhood. He napped in his bassinet in the sun as recommended by the doctor because of the slight jaundice he still had.

We had many visitors, and I had very little sleep. My new baby loved to eat. He would wake up every two or three hours at night to nurse. He also ate every two hours during the day. He was a little piggy, and he was gaining weight and some healthy rolls on his little body.

That summer, we went back to my hometown for my cousin's wedding shower. Kaden and I did the ninety-minute drive earlier that day. Brett and I had planned to travel separately. I forgot Kaden's entire overnight bag! It made me anxious about packing for him and forgetting something after that. It's amazing how the mind can play tricks on you. At least I did not forget his diaper bag. At least I did not forget my baby.

During my pregnancy, I had visions of walking around with my baby sleeping in his stroller while I listened to the birds and enjoyed every moment of summer and sunshine. The reality was my baby hated his stroller. The only walking I got was when he would go in the snuggly for twenty minutes.

That fall, Kaden and I developed a routine. I was getting some sleep at night and napping when Kaden did during the day to compensate. We decided to baptize Kaden in the faith of the United Church. Although we do not go to church, if we had to choose a religion, we would choose United. Getting your baby baptized seems like the thing to do when you have a baby. We were fortunate that Kaden would receive his blessing in Brett's hometown United Church. We each chose a sibling to be Kaden's godparents.

It was a beautiful baptism with immediate family and a few friends. We were happy to have it happen in the church that Brett had attended regularly as a kid. The minister was a kind woman who used seashells to place the water on Kaden's head. We got to keep the seashell, which I thought was a beautiful and symbolic gift for us.

That winter—due to lack of sleep, lack of exercise, and seasonal affective disorder—I became increasingly depressed. I suffer from seasonal affective disorder every year. That year, I had full-blown postpartum depression and anxiety. It is not a fun place to be. I was nursing and opted to go to counseling to deal with my emotions. I ate well and tried to get as much sleep as I could.

Nursing Kaden was very important to me. I declined taking medication for depression and anxiety. I had regular contact with my doctor to monitor how I was feeling and coping. There are times that women need medications. I believe—on a professional and personal note—that a woman needs to consult with her doctor if she is feeling depressed after having her baby. It is common for women to get postpartum depression.

Going to the grocery store with my new baby would cause me anxiety. Kaden hated his car seat and would cry the entire drive. I got to the point where I only went to a smaller grocery store. I also shopped in the evenings while

Brett was home with Kaden. Grocery shopping became enjoyable this way. I had a 1.5-hour window due to my nursing schedule and my son's refusal to take a bottle of breast milk or formula.

Kaden was six months old, and I was still nursing him every two or three hours at night. I was still in a "new-mom phase." My mom approached me and told me the baby could sleep through the night. She helped me take away a nighttime feeding by getting up when Kaden would awaken for his nighttime snack. Grandma would kindly offer him a bottle of water. This lasted a few nights, and my baby would finally sleep for six or eight hours. I felt like a new woman. It is amazing what sleep does for the energy and happiness level in a new mom.

I began attending a mom and tot group every week. It was nice to take a shower and do my hair for that group. It got us out of the house; the other moms wanted to gush over how cute and smart their babies were too. The same wonderful woman, Sheila, whom we had for our prenatal classes, ran this group as well. She mentioned that she would be beginning a postpartum support group soon. I needed it badly, however I did not put up my hand in front of everyone to maintain the idea that I was doing as well as everyone else.

I have no shame in being a counseling junkie. However, I was carrying shame about having postpartum depression. I knew I wanted to release it somehow. As a social worker, it would be hypocritical to not believe in counseling to resolve any trials in my life.

Kaden and I began attending the postpartum support group with Sheila. I faced my depression and anxiety with other moms who were having the same feelings. I felt normal again. We loved and adored our babies, but becoming a new mother was an adjustment.

The group counseling helped greatly. It made me feel normal again. It was comforting to talk with others who could relate to me. It was as if they were telling my story;

I shared my own thoughts too. I felt connected to these other mothers.

I am a support group junkie as well. I bear no shame in saying this either. I can let down my guard, allow myself to talk about everything I am carrying, and release it. Without talking, all the thoughts and emotions get tangled up in an indestructible knot within my brain. It messes with my psyche. There was never any judgment in the group because everyone was going through the same emotions and pain. I was understood, and it felt amazing. My support group played an instrumental role in my self-healing and slaying the dragon of postpartum depression that was on my back.

It can be difficult to explain what postpartum depression is. There are many great books that provide valuable information on this topic.

I wrote a poem to thank the other moms and Sheila. She always knew what to say. The women I met there had the courage to help themselves, and in doing that, they helped me.

Silver Lining

When they say, "Walk a mile in my shoes,"
We can say, "Yes, I have—and I have survived the war."
When we think and feel like we are back in a war zone,
We can say, "No, I have the ammunition to win this."

I will call on you—the ones who know the pain, the anguish, the anger, the guilt, the tears, the numbness, the chaos, the craziness, the madness, and eventually the peacefulness. If only for one minute, one hour, one day, or one week. We know, and we remember how we went there—how we found our peacefulness. If you forget, reach out for a hand that can tell you how to find it again. Though we have never been to war per se, I feel we have won the battle. Though there may be dark days ahead that are filled with rain, after the rain, there is sunshine. With help, if we look, maybe we can find our rainbow again. You women have been my silver lining. This is my thanks to you. Pamela.

The group ended, but it will always remain one of the best experiences of my life. The group came at a time when I was so lost, but I found myself again in the eyes of those mothers and Sheila. Thank you for showing me the way back to myself.

Sheila gave the best advice. She told us many people would tell us what to do and what not to do with our babies. When new mothers hear well-meaning advice, she told us to "smile politely, close our doors after they left," and "do whatever we wanted." It was nice to be given permission to do what we felt was right for our families. Her advice was always in the back of my mind when I was getting certain tips from "well-meaning" people.

I was still nursing and kept in regular contact with my doctor. I was able to beat postpartum depression with the help of many women. It is amazing how women can empower and inspire one another, especially when life is tough.

Our first Christmas with Kaden was amazing. The lucky kid got to wear an elf outfit that said "Baby's First Christmas." The joy a child brings to that festive time of year is precious—even if the baby is only six months old and only cares about the wrapping paper and bows and not the new present I had agonized over getting him. I debated if it was better to get an educational gift or a fun gift for Kaden. It ended up being a fun and magical time, regardless of the gift we bought.

After Christmas, Brett's beloved Granny got an infection and was admitted to the hospital. We went to see her and be with Brett's mom and his family. It was her time to go. She passed away on January 3, 2004. It was the first time I had seen my husband cry.

Granny's absence left such a hole in everyone's hearts. She was special and had seen Brett and his brothers almost daily as they grew up. The first time I met Granny, she was on the phone with her daughter. She said, "I better go now. Brett and his woman are here." I looked at Brett, and we exchanged smiles. I always teased him about being "his woman" after that.

She loved to play the game Trouble with us—probably because she always won. When Kaden came along, she was so happy for us. Like any good great-grandma, she thought Kaden was very smart. Of course we could not agree more. Everyone was mourning and trying to move forward with their grief and a life without Granny in it.

Winter turned into spring, and our baby was not crawling yet. It could be partly because we carried him everywhere. He did learn to walk in May at eleven months old. That same weekend, Kaden figured out crawling. Every kid is different, and if he did not crawl before walking, was it going to have a huge impact on his life? Would it affect his brain functioning and his ability to learn? I highly doubt it, but time will tell.

During my maternity leave, I was quite stressed about who would take care of Kaden when I returned to work. I was overprotective from my career as a social worker, and I knew a lot from experience.

I made a list of questions to ask potential caregivers: Are you licensed? How do you discipline? What are the foods you will be providing? Are you a pedophile? Have you been convicted of a felony? Will you hit my child? What are your strategies for encouraging self-esteem and self-growth for the children in your care?

Would they tell me the truth? Would a pedophile confess dark secrets to me? There was no video camera set up for me to watch how they cared for my child all day. I was praying for help.

My best friend, Jenna and I had a conversation a few days later. Her mom had offered to take care of Kaden when I went back to work. As Jenna talked, I was in shock. I had not been sleeping for several nights, as I was so concerned about returning back to work. I was afraid to leave my baby with a stranger. God had answered my prayers. I said, "Yes! Are you kidding me?"

It was going to make returning to work a lot easier. Kaden would be loved and cared for by someone I knew and trusted wholeheartedly.

Brett also thought it was amazing. I called Jessie and cried with relief as we discussed childcare for Kaden. I returned to work in July. Jessie watched Kaden in our home every morning. She lived around the block and would come over at seven thirty. Kaden was usually still sleeping when I left. It could not have been easier or more perfect for our family.

Jessie was another earth angel. She adored Kaden and was like another grandma to him. Returning to work was very difficult for me. I would not have left him with a stranger, but I had to return to work for financial reasons. I will forever cherish Jessie for this gift she has given our family.

A new routine began. If Kaden were awake when I left in the morning, he would cry as I hugged and kissed him good-bye. Even after several months, Kaden would still get upset. As I drove to work, I would cry as sharp pangs of guilt engulfed my heart. I would call home as soon as I stepped into my office. Kaden's crying would stop as soon as the door was closed and I was out of sight. That little turkey had me so wrapped around his little finger that I could not see straight. I would say silent prayers to God and hope my son was not working with a social worker in fifteen years because I was not home with him during this important time in his young life.

It was difficult to decide what to do as a woman. I had such a strong urge to be home with Kaden. I also felt it was important to have my own career. I wanted to provide for myself financially and contribute to our family. I went back to work part-time, which was a perfect fit for us.

Life became busy and hectic, but we had a routine. We adjusted to the big changes of having a child. We wondered what we did before with all the free time—and all the time in the world to sleep.

Becoming a parent changed our lives. I was in awe of Kaden. His beautiful face and wonderful personality had both Brett and I hooked.

CHAPTER 6

Garret ... My Soul Brother

Summer flew by, and we headed into the season of fall. Harvest was in full swing, and the leaves on the trees were changing colors. There was a feeling of urgency in the air. We needed to be outside to feel the warmth of the sun on our faces before winter settled in.

The farmers were harvesting their crops, and rural towns were buzzing with excitement. In September, I visited my family and had the opportunity to catch up with my first cousin and "my soul brother" Garret.

He needed a ride to the field to change vehicles. I adored him, and he was the only person who called me "Pammy" besides his mom. Garret was nine months younger than me, and I had taken him under my wing since I could walk.

Our mothers were sisters. These sisters had each married their high school sweethearts in the month of October after graduating from high school. They both started families thereafter. Each of them had taken turns having babies each year. There were seven of us cousins. Even though we were first cousins, it felt more like one big family when we were together. Garret had an older sister who was one year older than me and she was the first grandchild in the family. He was the first grandson on our side of the family.

Garret was gentle, quiet, sweet, mischievous, and kind. His heart was the size of the universe. He was a proud husband and an even prouder father of two girls. He had a beautiful two-year-old daughter and a new baby girl, almost three months old. We had a great visit, and he commented how life was so hectic right then. He hardly saw his family, but he was planning to relax after harvest and spend time with "his girls."

I gave him a great big hug. I drove back to the city with Kaden that night. We got back into our routine, and life was busy. We planned to go to Mexico for Christmas since my middle sister was getting married there.

We headed to bed early on weekdays because of work. I was in a deep, sound sleep when the phone rang at midnight on October 3, 2003. I woke with tightness in my chest and a pain in my stomach. I knew something was wrong.

My mom said, "I have bad news. There was an accident. Garret has died."

My body went into shock. I couldn't believe the words I was hearing. A part of me knew it was the truth. I hung up the phone, packed a bag, and rode with my uncle to be with our family.

We arrived at my aunt and uncle's home in the middle of the night and tried to be as helpful as we could while offering sympathy. Everyone was reeling with shock and crying. Pain was everyone's new reality. Life would go on without Garret in it.

I first approached my aunty, hugged her, and told her how sorry I was.

She said, "Make sure you hold on tight to your son because you never know what will happen."

Her pain was so raw. I nodded and said, "Okay."

Prayers and a Catholic funeral were planned. Everything was going so fast. The priest had difficulty with the service as well. He loved Garret and considered him a friend. Shock flooded that small town, and the community pulled together to help the family harvest their crops.

Life would never be the same again for those of us close to Garret. Many waded through the pain of losing a husband, father, son, nephew, brother, cousin, and friend.

I turned thirty on October 20—seventeen days after Garret went to heaven. I clearly remember blowing out my candles. All I could think was that Garret would never turn thirty. The grief was difficult. I could not find the gratitude in the gift that I got to turn thirty. Live each moment! This is what grief does to you. Even though you may be alive and well on the inside, you do not feel that way. The thoughts and pain in your chest do not scream, "Thank you for my birthday." Instead the words clanking around in my brain were, "Why did he have to die?"

There will never be another person in my life like him. He was my cousin through blood, but he was my little brother on a soul level. I was one grade higher in school. Growing up, I was either in a classroom with his older sister or with him.

I remember his kindness, hearty chuckle, and the twinkle in his eye when he was smiling or laughing. I remember playing basketball together as kids and kicking Garret's butt. Actually, it was pretty even for wins and losses if my memory serves me correctly.

I can see us riding the go-cart and driving into the edge of the garage. We played Ping-Pong and Pac-Man and Mario Brothers in the basement. We rode bikes, took swimming lessons together, and hung out together on weekends.

My friends ran against Garret for class president in grade five and six. Garret's political campaign consisted of promising popcorn for everyone in the classes if he won. He won by one or two votes. My campaign team asked who I had voted for. I was truthful and said, "Garret." They were so mad at me but how could I vote for anyone but Garret.

He was true to his word and came to school the following day with black garbage bags full of brown paper bags of popcorn that he handed out to everyone. Integrity is a hot commodity, and that is what he always had. I was always curious about how long it took to make all that popcorn.

Garret always called me "Pammy." I have had a few friends say it, but it is not at all like when Garret would say it. That name died the day that Garret died. My aunty still calls me it sometimes, and it reminds me of my childhood connection to them.

I had many heart-to-hearts with Garret when he was alive—and even now when I need to tell him something. I know he is with me. He fell hopelessly in love with his wife at university. He fell twice as hard for his daughters.

I remember watching him feed his firstborn. She was just under five pounds and so tiny. He was so gentle and careful with her. He was the first of the cousins to become a parent.

If I knew that I would not see Garret again, I would have asked about his favorite things and memories. There are a few important lessons from this for me: Tell the people you love all the wonderful things you love about them. Chat about all the good times and fond memories you have of your times together. Make more memories that are happy and wonderful.

I would have thanked Garret for being my little brother. I would have played "Cotton Eyed Joe" and had him two-step with me in the field like we did during our university days.

I would have hugged him harder and said, "I love you like no other." I know he knew that though. I learned that someone you love could be gone in a moment. I try to be kind and love the ones I love in earnest.

Garret, I know you are here with us. I love you like no other. I feel like you are smiling at me. Your beautiful smile and charming wit live on in all my memories of you. Save a chair for me at your breakfast table for when we meet again. I looked forward to watching you break apart your bacon and put the pieces on your over-easy eggs, applying pepper, and eating it with toast.

I can see the pure satisfaction on your face as you enjoy this. You had a knack for enjoying the simple things in life. What a gift that was. After brunch together, get your dancing shoes on because we are going to two-step or polka to "The Good Die Young." I may even let you lead this time.

The reality is that life is going on around you when you have lost someone you love deeply. The week after Garret's funeral was Thanksgiving. Brett's brother was getting married too. Six days after the news—and the day after the funeral—I had to put a smile on my face and pretend life was great. Brett and I were both in the wedding party. I was happy for the couple. I adored my new sister-in-law, but I was grief-stricken.

The phrase "life goes on" really hit home for me that weekend. Life does go on—even when you are crying inside and desperately want the world to stop. It was a beautiful wedding, and I was able to keep it together and stay in the moment.

The following weekend, I had to fly out to be in another wedding party. Raya had fallen in love with her hockey coach, and they were getting married. Kent was wonderful to her son and stepped in to be a wonderful dad. I could not have been happier for Raya. Even though I was happy for them, there was a pain in my chest and a lump in my throat. It was nice to come full circle and see that Raya had found happiness again after the tragic loss of Kohen.

I still felt like crying all the time, but I was able to hold it in for that wedding celebration too. Thank you, God and angels, for the gift of shock and numbness. I completely disassociated from my grief to be present in those moments.

My sister was getting married on December 23 in the Mayan Riviera. With our toddler in tow, we were off to Mexico. It was an amazing trip, and all of the bride and groom's immediate family attended.

Kaden would not allow his aunty to dance with her new husband. Deanna had lived with us for nine months while completing her education degree. Kaden had grown quite attached to her and was quite possessive of his aunty. As the only baby, he ran the show wherever he went. He was not nicknamed King Kaden for nothing!

We returned home and had our first big family celebration without Garret in January. The newly married had a big dance to celebrate their nuptials. I knew Garret was there in spirit, but it was painful to not have him there in body. He would have danced with the bride, my lovely sister. Garret and Deanna were roommates in university and were very close. Many of their mutual university friends were celebrating with us.

Garret was so missed and had touched so many people's lives. Seeing his young widow with her small daughters, fatherless, was heartbreaking. Sometimes it is hard not to feel like life is cruel.

CHAPTER 7
Baby Number Two

O ur fun trip to Mexico is behind us and hopefully winter is going to be gone soon. Kaden has just past the eighteen-month mark, and we were ready to have a second child.

I had been working full-time for six months, and Kaden had settled in with Jessie. I was enjoying working with teenagers and their parents. Brett was still doing transportation, but he was thinking about other job opportunities.

As quickly as we decided to try, we were pregnant. It all began on February 5. We conceived right away. As with most things that you are doing for the second time, you don't need advice. This pregnancy I did not read any books, and we did not take the prenatal classes.

Two of my closest friends from school were pregnant and their babies were due around the same time. In no time at all, I was twenty weeks pregnant. We were driving to our first ultrasound appointment and we were just as excited about this baby as we were with Kaden. Brett and I decided that we wanted to find out the sex of the baby this time. It was nice to be surprised with Kaden, but this time we wanted to know. We were planning to have three children so we could be surprised again with the last baby if we didn't like knowing this time around.

During the ultrasound, we asked the technician to write down what we were having. She knew we had a son already. We bragged about Kaden while she checked out the beautiful baby I was carrying. I am amazed by ultrasounds, and I loved watching the baby on the screen. I always ask the technician to make sure I can see the screen fully. I have been blessed with wonderful technicians who are always so helpful and accommodating. After it was over she handed us a sealed envelope and smiled at us as she said good-bye.

Brett drove me back to work. I put the envelope in the glove box of the car, as I could not hold it. I knew the words in that envelope would change my life. Neither Brett nor I cared what the sex of the baby was going to be. I really felt a strong pull toward a girl. I felt like I was carrying differently than I had with Kaden.

We chatted for a few more minutes, but we could not wait any longer. Brett pulled into the parking lot beside the park where our wedding pictures were taken. It was perfect! It was so crazy how things lined up for us.

My heart began to race. A smile tugged at the corners of my mouth. I tore open the envelope and read the magical words. These words were going to change our lives.

My heart quickened and my mind raced. I was 99 percent confident we were having a girl. The thoughts were racing through my mind. Pink or blue, pink or blue, pink, pink, pink, pink?

"Congratulations on a little brother for Kaden."

Oh my goodness ... another boy! Blue, blue, blue, blue!

I was surprised and excited. I already adored Kaden! I could see the two of them together—just like Brett and his brothers. From that moment on, all I saw was our two boys playing together, roughhousing, and even fighting at times. *Boys will be boys*, I thought to myself. My mind instantly created the family that was going to be. I could see it in my mind's eye, and it was perfect. I could almost touch the two of them if I closed my eyes. I could feel their presence when I put my hand on my stomach. I felt the baby boy growing within my womb. Would this baby boy look like Brett? Kaden looked just like me so maybe this baby would look just like his Daddy!

I felt peaceful and serene—as though life could not get any better. I imagined a beautiful mountain with softly fallen snow and a rising sun shining brightly under a perfect rainbow. My heart was overflowing with joy.

Soon I would have my two boys. We would play baseball and soccer together. We would fish and swim like great warriors. We would watch them play Timbit hockey. He shoots—he scores. The Larocque brothers!

We would see them sharing brotherly love and companionship. Look at the Larocque brothers. Aren't they cute and adorable? They grow older, stronger, and more handsome everyday. I dreamed about my family and my boys.

We chose to keep it a secret from everyone, but it felt so amazing to know we would have another son. I could not help but smile. Kaden was as cute, funny, and smart as ever. There was nothing he could do that we did not think was amazing. Soon we would have two sons to gush over.

For the first time, I went alone for my regular weekly checkup with my family doctor about a week after our ultrasound. I told Brett that he could stay at work. She would be transferring my file after this visit to the ob-gyn I had seen for my pregnancy with Kaden.

I was excited to tell my doctor our good news. I waited for the usual prenatal questions from my doctor: How are you feeling? Do you have any concerns since we last met? How is the weight gain?

I could sense something was not right when she came in the room and sat down. She looked directly into my eyes and stated that the ultrasound results had found cysts on the baby's brain. She kindly gave me the rest of the news in a soothing and calm voice. There was concern that the baby had Trisomy 18. I heard the words she was saying, but I was finding it hard to comprehend. Dread filled my heart.

She told me we had just missed the time frame to measure the circumference of the baby's head, which was another sign of that condition. At the eighteen-week mark, they could use that as a marker to help decide if the baby had this condition or not, but our baby was twenty weeks old. *At the ultrasound, had the technician been quiet?* It did seem to take longer than the ultrasound that I had with Kaden at twenty weeks. We were two weeks past this testing procedure.

The only option was to wait eight weeks and have another ultrasound to find out if the cysts were still there. I began crying, wishing Brett was there with me. I heard my doctor's voice and forced myself to listen and concentrate. The good news was that the baby's forearms were normal. If they were abnormal, it would have been another sign of Trisomy 18. If my baby had the condition, than the pregnancy may not progress to full term. The baby could die inside the womb. If my baby were born, he would not live long. Those were harsh words to hear. Doctors don't have the easiest jobs either. Relaying that news to a hormonal mother would not be on my list of enjoyable experiences. My news to tell her about having a boy had lost its excitement. I did tell her through my tears at the end of the appointment that I was carrying a baby boy.

I left the doctor's office and called Brett. I tried to keep my composure as I got the words out through my tears. Brett was quiet as I am sure he was in shock. He told me that he would meet me at home shortly. Next I called work and spoke to my assistant supervisor. I was unable to maintain any emotional control. I was crying as I repeated the words for the second time in five minutes.

I told her there might be something wrong with my baby. I heard myself say the words "Trisomy 18." I let her know I could not go back to work for the remainder of the afternoon. She was very supportive of my decision. She was kind and compassionate. She had two young children, and I knew her heart went out to me.

I walked in the door and relayed the news to my mother-in-law who was taking care of Kaden for the day. She was very positive and said there would be nothing wrong with our baby as she hugged me. I prayed she was right and hoped time would tell.

Many thoughts were going through my head. I googled Trisomy 18 on my computer even though my doctor told me not to look it up on the Internet. It was not fun to read, but something inside me wanted an answer. I talked to God and prayed for a miracle for my baby—and a miracle for us.

I returned to work the following day. I had slept well and felt capable of going back. The uncertainty of the situation was teaching me to let go and let God deal with my worries. The next eight weeks felt very long for me. I was grateful for my work and my family.

After two long months, we drove to the hospital for the ultrasound. We would find out what we had been fearful of. The threat of our baby having Trisomy 18 was like having a dark cloud following us wherever we went. At any moment, it could strike us like a lightning bolt and end the life of the baby I was carrying.

I was hooked up to the machine, and the lab technician rubbed the cold gel on my tummy. We were fortunate to see our baby in 3-D. Our baby boy was smiling. His face was so beautiful and delicate. He was absolutely gorgeous! That smile warmed my heart. For a moment, I forgot why we were there and enjoyed the moment. Seeing our baby for the first time in 3-D was amazing!

The lab technician had never seen a baby smiling in the womb before. This child was special. There was no doubt in my mind that he was going to be okay. He was smiling to give his momma a sign!

The next few moments were monumental. She relayed to us that there were no cysts in the brain that she could find. That was a happy day! It was a miracle. The doctor came in and told us the same news. In the blink of an eye, our situation had changed. There were no concerns with our baby boy having Trisomy 18. Smooth sailing was ahead. He would live! I wanted to dance and jump for joy, but I smiled instead as tears of relief flooded my eyes. Happiness filled me to the very core of my existence.

It was a day for rejoicing. My life was back on track, and I could have my dreams again of life with our two boys. The death sentence of Trisomy 18 for our son had been lifted. The dark cloud in my mind had lifted in that moment as well. I felt exhilaration in my heart! My baby was going to be all right. He was going to live! Thank you, God, for this miracle.

I was not regretful that we found out we were having another boy. It was the opposite. I was filled with wonder and love. I knew my baby so deeply, especially after thinking he would die from that rare condition. I already felt the deepest bond with my second son. Now we needed to name him.

The summer Kaden was born, I had watched a show with a character named Reichen. I loved the name, but I changed the spelling of it to "Ryken." I googled the meaning of it: which was *champion*. Our son was a champion, especially after the past few months. Sold. I loved his name!

However, Brett did not love the name, but the meaning behind the name sealed the deal for me. When I found out that Ryken meant *champion*, I was hooked. I knew it would be his name. I even started to call him Ryken when I touched my stomach or felt him kick.

Like any good wife, I challenged Brett to find a name. He had to find a first name and a second name to go with it. I liked Addison for a middle name. We would talk about a different name for our baby when he found one he liked. If Brett could not find a suitable name, then my name would win. Brett agreed, and the name of our baby remained undecided.

In June, Brett got a new job that was forty-five minutes away. We would have to move to a smaller city of thirty thousand people. It did not bother me since I was planning to take the full maternity leave allowed, which was one year. I would figure out my commute to my job later on.

I wrote a list for our house that included three bedrooms on the main floor, a thousand-square-foot bungalow, and a finished basement with a bedroom, a big yard, and a two-car garage. The price for the house had to be around $120,000.

I was looking at houses on the computer and saw a house that had just come onto the market. It was a three-bedroom bungalow for $126,900. The property had a yard the size of a small football field and a double detached garage. It was 912 square feet on each floor and had a finished basement with a spare room.

When I get excited I am not the kind of person to sit and wait. Even though it was just after nine o'clock in the evening, I picked up the phone and called the number. The owner answered right away. They were selling privately, and it had just been listed that evening. Arrangements were made for the following evening at six thirty to take a look at it. I asked Jessie if she would come with Kaden and me. Brett was out of town for the week with his new job.

The three of us parked across the street from the house. It was perfect for us. I knew we were going to buy it. There were many other people interested in the house as well. They were lined up on the driveway, waiting to look at it after our turn.

I was the first person to call and schedule a viewing. Kaden was so cute—and I was six months pregnant—and the owner agreed to give me the night to talk with Brett and decide on it. As we were walking out the door, another family was walking in to view the house. I knew in my heart that it was ours. I had no concern that someone else would buy it. I didn't mind if they took a look at my new home!

I was very grateful the owners gave me the night to talk with Brett. We drove back the following evening again with Brett this time. The energy of the home felt so good, and the owners were wonderful. Brett got to take a look around and was as excited as I was. Brett was impressed with the yard and the garage. There was a long driveway for Kaden to play hockey and ride his bike on.

We finalized the purchase of the house and took possession on October 1. It was one month before my due date. Everything in my life was running smoothly. I was feeling at peace and had no trepidation about moving. In comparison to the possibility of our baby having a rare condition and dying, moving to a new city was going to be a piece of cake.

We had a family reunion on my dad's side in July. The reunions were held every five years and had begun when I was fifteen. Brett and I went to the one in 2000. This time, I was pregnant and had a two year old. At the next reunion, my boys would be seven and four. I would get to show off my new baby to everyone—even though he would be a preschooler. This time we had our sunshine Kaden to show off and a pregnant belly. We would keep the family members guessing what we had for the next family reunion in 5 years time.

There were more than 250 people, and I did not even know everyone. At big family reunions, everyone sticks with the people they already know. There is not a lot of getting to know other family members, which is the whole point. You do get the chance to connect with people you really want to visit. I tried to meet some new people, spend time with my favorites, visit my sisters, and chase after a toddler, while being 6 months pregnant. I felt like I was pulled in a million directions. It was a great time though. The weekend flew by, and the reunion was a lot of fun.

Next on our "to do" list was to sell our old home. Kaden went with my mom for the weekend at the farm, and we prepared our home for pictures for the website and showings. It was the first time we had been away from Kaden in his life. We were very busy, but we missed him greatly. He did well on his sleepover with his grandma and grandpa.

Our house sold within a month. Brett was away at work, and I had a bidding war on my hands. Two parties were negotiating to buy our house. The pregnancy was going by very fast, and I was really busy. I was able to handle the stress by going to the gym during my lunch breaks and walking daily. I was vigilant about eating healthily and getting enough sleep. I was looking forward to my new baby and time at home with Kaden. Life was really great. I enjoyed my job and the families I was working with. My last day before maternity leave was September 26.

I wanted to get the house unpacked as quickly as possible since we had a new baby coming. It was the second time we had moved, and we had lots of help. I was thirty-six weeks pregnant, and there was definitely no lifting any boxes for me. I was happy to boss everyone around. It worked out great.

The dilemma was choosing the colors for the inside of our new house. As a Libra, too many choices did not help. I was able to decide on colors with the help of my husband. Brett's dad helped with the painting. He is very good at it and lent out his talent to our walls.

We were settling in quite well. As we unpacked and hung pictures on the walls, we were anxiously awaiting the birth of the second child and grandchild into the family. We were ready. After our scare, he was even more special to us. We were glad that brief nightmare had passed.

I did not write down my birth plan. It was lodged in my mind. I had the birth thing sorted out the second time around. We were pros. I would get an epidural as soon as I walked in the door. I had a doula, and we got along amazingly. She was perfect for me. She would hold my legs so Brett would not have to.

I continued my nesting activities and got back into a routine with Kaden. We still napped during the afternoons. I was not sleeping so well since the baby did a lot of kicking. I told Brett that the baby had his long legs.

CHAPTER 8

A Champion Is Born

A t 3:30 a.m. on October 18 my water broke. There was not a lot of water like I had with Kaden, but I knew it had broken. I stayed awake beside Brett, and he slept peacefully until seven. I woke him up and notified him that my water had broke and than called my mom. The day had finally come. Our second son would arrive soon—healthy and alive. As I rested my hand on my stomach, our little boy kicked out to me as if to say, "I'll see you soon, Mommy." I smiled down at my baby and thought, *Can't wait, Ryken.* Brett still had no name picked out. It was looking like I was going to win.

Since I knew what to expect with labor and delivery, I was a bit fearful. I would have an epidural as soon as I entered the ward, which took away some of my fear. I had no contractions or labor pains yet but knew they would come soon enough.

Brett took the day off, and my parents would drive the ninety minutes to our home to pick up Kaden and take him to their farm. They were at our home by nine. We chatted briefly and went to the big city to have our baby.

I was admitted to labor and delivery, and it was confirmed that my water had indeed broken. A few weeks earlier, I had been shopping and was convinced my water had broken. I went to the hospital, but I had peed my pants from the pressure of the baby's head on my bladder. I think the nurse was trying to make me feel better. It was slightly embarrassing, but I was able to get over it. In a second pregnancy, you learn to lighten up a bit.

Once I was admitted to labor and delivery, I explained my birth plan very assertively to my nurse. I had it memorized. I looked her in the eye and said, "I want an epidural. When can I get my epidural?"

Her response to me was when I was dilated between four and six centimeters, I could get one.

According to my birth plan, this baby would not have jaundice—and we would go home right away. The second time around was going to be easy. I could not wait to meet our second son and see what he looked like. I loved knowing the sex of the baby. It was just as exciting for me to know what we were having as it was not knowing. I was very happy we did not find out with Kaden, and I was very thankful we had found out we were having a boy the second time around. I wondered what we would do with the next pregnancy.

There were so many thoughts running through my mind. I truly loved little boys. I grew up with sisters, and boys are their own breed. They play, have fun, and capture your heart at the same time.

My body decided not to begin having contractions on its own. The doctor gave me a few hours to see what my body would do. By late afternoon, he decided to induce me. They hooked me up to a baby monitor, and the baby's heartbeat was great.

My doula arrived that evening to help us. The induction became painful quite quickly. It was completely different than my induction with Kaden. I asked for the epidural, and the nurse checked me. I was five centimeters dilated, and they called the anesthesiologist.

The induction had begun at four o'clock. The first part of my labor lasted three hours. The labor pains were hard and fast. They were a lot more painful than I remembered. There was no suggestion of an exercise ball.

I was having trouble breathing during the contractions. I felt like I was going to die. There was no time to catch my breath between contractions. *I did say epidural right? Where is the anesthesiologist? Help me! I just need something to get rid of this pain!* My body was riddled with jabbing shots of agony.

My doula was beside the bed, and I tried to talk to her, but it was difficult. Brett was holding my hand. I can only imagine how it feels to watch the woman you love go through such pain and anguish. *Those poor men. Yeah, right! I need an epidural now!*

My day shift nurse walked into the room. They were changing shifts, and she wanted to wish me luck. It was seven twenty, and I had just been told that I was not getting an epidural. It was too late for one.

I had just entered the second stage of labor. I still had a hard time catching my breath. I grabbed her hand, looked directly into her eyes, and begged her not to leave. "You can't leave me. Please don't leave me!"

She said, "Okay. I will stay with you." She sat down beside me and held my hand.

I had no idea where my doula was, and the pain was unbearable.

Brett was at the top of the bed, but I could not see him. The nurse was my voice of reason and calm. The contractions were fast, hard, excruciating. They hit me one after another, showing no mercy.

I could feel the baby ripping through my body. I let out a scream that I did not recognize as mine. Then, I felt nothing. The pain was gone. I was gone. All of a sudden, I was floating quietly and softly. The pain disappeared into thin air.

I rested in the stillness. My body no longer hurt. The agony ceased to exist. The screaming was so loud. I did not know who I was. I had passed the threshold of what I could tolerate. I had separated from myself. I was no longer in my own body.

I felt something wet and warm. The nurse grabbed my hand and placed it directly on the baby's head. "There's the baby's head, Pam!"

I feel a whoosh as my soul decided to go back into my body.

"You need to push."

I felt the energy in my hand. Underneath my fingers, my baby's head was hard and wet. I felt my soul slam back into my body. I was fully aware of the pain, and the quietness was gone.

The doctor's calm presence reassured me. My nurse guiding me with her words gave me the much needed encouragement to push.

I was in full-blown, excruciating labor and pushing hard. The short reprieve gave me a renewed strength to continue. I was back in the game of life, and the baby was finally coming out. I was able to focus, and my screaming stopped.

With the next few pushes, our beautiful baby was out and placed on my chest. After twenty-five minutes of painstakingly hard labor, our beautiful son was born. In twenty minutes, I went from five to ten centimeters and pushing the baby out.

The third stage of labor lasted four minutes. At seven forty-five, our son emerged into this world. I felt such a relief that it was finally over. The pain disappeared immediately.

I looked at my beautiful son for the first time. Even though I had seen him on the screen, there was no comparison to the real thing. It was like looking into the face of an angel. He had soft, blond, wispy hair, delicate features, and beautiful blue eyes. I was hopelessly in love again. Instantaneously, just like with Kaden.

I stared into his eyes, and my heart was enveloped in profound love. The day is finally here. Our beautiful little boy had finally arrived.

Our second son was the spitting image of Brett. He really did not look anything like Kaden. His skin was pinker and fairer—just like Brett's. His blue eyes, blond hair, long legs, and long torso were replicas of Brett's baby pictures. Genetics fascinates me. Kaden looked so much like me that I thought it was nice to have another child that looked like his daddy.

As I counted his ten little fingers and ten little toes, I stopped at his left foot. The toe right next to his baby toe looked like it was out of place. It was tucked behind his middle toe. The doctors and nurses must not have noticed it, and if they had, it must not be a concern. I never worried about my baby's fingers and toes during my pregnancy. Now I was concerned about his foot and his ability to walk. If he were anything like Kaden, he would be walking before he was a year old. I didn't want him to have any issues with his first steps. I tucked away my concern and would chat with the doctor at a later time.

Other than this nagging thought, I felt so good. We were so excited. I nursed my new baby for the first time, and he latched on perfectly. I knew what I was doing the second time around. He was a quick learner and so smart. What an amazing little person you are!

Our new bundle of joy weighed in at seven pounds and ten ounces and measured 21⅝ inches. The nurse had noticed that he was favoring his right arm. Other than that, he appeared fine with an Apgar score of nine after the first minute and nine again after five minutes. Brett went with him for his first bath.

I felt amazing. I delivered the placenta intact with a three-vessel cord. I had a small, first-degree perineal tear, which was sutured. This was nothing like my delivery of Kaden! The burning ring of fire was gone, and I had hardly any stitches. I felt fantastic.

When Brett and the baby returned, we chatted with our doula and gushed over our new son. I looked over at Brett and said, "What are we naming him?"

Brett replied, "We can name him Ryken. You deserve to name him after that painful labor."

He was right. I was so excited. I absolutely loved the name Ryken Addison Larocque.

I peered down at the treasure and said, "Hello Ryken Addison." I kissed his smooth cheek and snuggled him close to my neck. *Welcome to the world, my precious son. I love you so much already. We are both champions for surviving that birth. I feel like a champion for winning the choice to name our newest addition. Yeah, yeah, yeah. I am so happy!*

We began calling our parents and siblings to let them know about our newest addition. Our eyes were twinkling, and we were smiling. "It's a boy!"

"His name is Ryken Addison." We talked about his weight and length with such pride and joy. There was so much excitement in sharing the news of the birth, especially when no one knew the sex of the baby. Everyone was just as excited and happy as we were. Ryken was the second grandchild on either side.

At nine o'clock, we decided that Kaden could visit the following day. It would take over an hour to drive to the hospital. He was already in his pajamas and heading to bed. My parents would come after lunch and Kaden would finally meet his new brother. We had been preparing him for months about his new baby that was coming.

Our doula left, and Brett helped move us to a semiprivate room. He snuggled his new son for a while, and we had some alone time to talk about the craziness of the past few hours. I was beaming. Brett left around eleven o'clock and drove home. We kissed and hugged good-bye. We were happy and tired.

I nursed my beautiful son again and changed his diaper. I wrapped him up tightly and placed him in his bassinet. Ryken began to cry. I picked him up and snuggled him to my chest. He instantly stopped crying. Once I was confident he was asleep again, I would put him back in the bassinet. Within seconds, Ryken would begin to cry again.

I would start all over again, trying to get him back to sleep. We played that game for a few more minutes. Ryken would only remain calm and sleeping when he was snuggled into my chest.

My mother's intuition told me to let Ryken sleep with me. I placed him in the crook of my left arm and had him leaning on his right side. I said, "Snug as a bug in a rug." I peered down at my beautiful son in complete awe. There was such a mixture of love and joy at his safe arrival. My second son had finally arrived. It felt like I had been waiting for him for so long. He was healthy and sleeping peacefully in my arms. I fell asleep with a smile on my face.

We slept for hours, and Ryken did not make a sound. He would wake up every few hours, and I would nurse him. We would fall right back asleep together. Ryken was so content in my arms. I usually follow rules, but I was happy to sleep and snuggle my new bundle of joy. The nurse never reprimanded me either when she came in to see how we were doing.

It hurt my heart when he cried in his bassinet. He had wrapped me around his fingers within hours of his arrival. All the fear and trepidation during the pregnancy was worth that moment. Thank you, God, for Ryken. Thank you, thank you, thank you. I am beaming from the inside out.

The following morning, October 19, Brett arrived, coffee in hand, after a good night's sleep. On his way home the night before, he had stopped and helped a woman on the side of the highway. She had a flat tire, and Brett changed it for her. My husband is the kindest human being I have ever met and I have the privilege to be his wife.

When our family doctor met our new son, I grabbed my camera and took a few pictures of her with Ryken. Ryken was crying as she checked him over. When she held him up and changed his position, he would stop crying. She was able to assess that he had a broken collarbone on his left side. It must have been from the fast delivery. Other than that, Ryken was given a clean bill of health.

I understood why he would cry in the bassinet. The way I held him must have taken away the pressure on his broken clavicle. My poor, sweet baby. I am so thankful that I followed my mother's intuition last night and snuggled him with me for the night.

CHAPTER 9

Black Meconium Diaper

W e held our baby and gushed over him the morning after his arrival. He seemed to be doing okay even though he had a broken clavicle. My best friend stopped by to see us during her lunch break. I was so full of pride to show him off and introduce her to Ryken. As Jenna was holding and rocking Ryken, I relayed our birth story. She loved his name too!

We continued chatting and I changed Ryken's diaper. *Yeah!* He was pooping out the black meconium. I was so excited about it and began wiping at the tar-like substance that streaked his little bum.

I looked up into his sweet face to talk to him and commend him on what a good job his body was doing by getting that yucky stuff out. As I looked at his face, I noticed that Ryken's lips were blue. In that instant, a tightening in my stomach began. I asked Brett if he could get the nurse. Jenna came over to the bed. She had her own beautiful ten-month-old baby boy at home. She could feel my anxiety and tried to calm me down with reassuring words.

I finished up the diaper change, and a nurse arrived right away. She checked him and took Ryken to the nursery. Jenna gathered her coat to leave, and I told her I would let her know what was going on later as Brett and I followed the nurse and Ryken.

The nurse placed Ryken on a bassinet and began working on him. She said he was having a "dusky spell."

Brett and I stood back to the side and watched the nurse working on Ryken. She placed the oxygen around his mouth and nose, rubbed his back, and listened to his heartbeat.

All of a sudden, my parents were in the hallway with Kaden. We walked outside to greet them. Our little man looked so big now in comparison to Ryken. We exchanged congratulatory hugs with my parents and walked back to my room.

We gave Kaden the stuffed toy that Ryken had brought for him. The stuffed bunny was almost the same size as Kaden. Max was from Kaden's favorite television show "Max and Ruby." Kaden gave him a big hug and was happy with this new gift.

Siblings were not allowed in the nursery, so we could not introduce the brothers to each other yet. Kaden was so excited about his new rabbit that he did not seem to care where the new baby was. I wished Kaden could see Ryken to thank him and give him a kiss. I really wanted him to meet his new baby, but I tried to be patient.

I took my parents in to the nursery to meet Ryken. Brett and Kaden stayed together playing in the room with Max. As we approached the bassinet that held my baby the nurse was still working on him. Ryken is on his side, and she was rubbing his back. She was talking to him and trying to stimulate him. A monitor on his foot checked his oxygen levels.

I had a small knot of fear and anxiety in my stomach, but I willed it away. I did not understand what was going on with my baby. The nurse did not say anything but continued her routine with him.

My parents and I returned to my room and chatted with Kaden. He was as cute as ever, and I missed him so much. We had not seen him for almost forty-one hours. Kaden was giggling and having fun. I stayed for a few more minutes and went to see my baby down the hall. Kaden was doing fine, but I was not so sure about Ryken. I had to go to him.

My mom and I returned to the nursery. Ryken was getting continuous oxygen through nose tubes now. The nurse was focusing all of her attention on him and was very quiet.

This continued for the next few hours. Finally around 6 pm they admitted Ryken into the neonatal intensive care unit (NICU). They wheeled our baby down the hall without any explanation as to why. I am guessing that they don't know and my stomach began to hurt.

Kaden had left a few hours earlier with my parents. Brett and I decided to grab something to eat before heading down to the NICU. I was drawn to the gift store. As we entered a magnetic force was guiding me to the stuffed animals.

Within a moment I knew why. I saw the cutest light blue puppy. He had white around his mouth, nose, ears, and feet. His eyes were brown thread. He was perfect. I had to buy the puppy for Ryken. I felt he needed a little buddy in NICU. We paid for the puppy, headed to the cafeteria to eat quickly, and went upstairs to be with our baby.

We washed our hands, which we learned is standard protocol upon entering the NIC unit, than immediately went to find Ryken. The nurse told us he had remained the same. He was in the least serious part of neonatal. We thought it was a good sign and my stomach seemed to settle down.

I placed his puppy in the bassinet beside him, as I leaned down, and whispered, "Hello, Ryken. It's Mommy. I love you. Here is a new friend to keep you company when I can't be here with you. He is your very own special puppy." I kissed his soft cheek and held onto his tiny fingers. I stroked his little hand.

I asked a nurse about pumping. I had not nursed Ryken since lunch, and I was desperately in need of a pump. I wanted to make sure I had established my milk and did not want to have any blocked milk ducts. I had learned a lot from nursing Kaden.

I was shown to the small rooms set up specifically for mothers to pump in. There was a fridge and freezer to store the milk in after. I left Brett with Ryken to complete my task.

When I returned, I stood beside the bassinet and kept watch over my new charge. Ryken seemed to be twitching occasionally, and then his whole body jerked. It was very hard to watch. I told myself he was okay. He was just dreaming. I pushed away my concerns, stroked his body, and leaned down to whisper soothing words in his ear. I hoped it would bring him some comfort to hear my voice, at the very least, to know I was with him.

I sat down beside my baby. I was able to touch him, but I couldn't hold him. I stroked his hand. I needed Ryken to know I was there with him. I had hardly held my baby, and he had hardly nursed either.

I was at a loss for words. What was there to say? Nothing. I had many questions and no answers. Fear and anxiety began to sprout tiny roots in the pit of my stomach. Doubt gnawed at my brain. I had an upset stomach and felt shaky. I tried to stay positive. I stuffed my emotions inward and downward. I tried to focus on being present for Ryken and staying positive.

We were able to chat with one of the doctors. We asked why Ryken was turning blue and in the NIC unit now.

The answer we got was that he had been born so fast that they suspect cerebral edema or brain swelling. That was the cause of Ryken's lips turning blue and the dusky spells and why his breathing had slowed down. Once the swelling in his brain went down, he should be okay.

Those words were music to my ears—sweet, beautiful music. It made sense to both of us. No wonder his brain was swollen. His birth was traumatic. The news from the doctor was comforting.

Brett's parents arrived to meet their new grandbaby. A little while later, my dad and stepmom met their new grandson.

Ryken was lethargic and not showing much interest in eating. They gave him an IV for hydration. I began my routine of pumping in the small room with my sterile bag of pumping accessories. I hated to leave Ryken's side, but he would need to eat soon. It was my job to produce healthy milk for my baby.

The first time I pumped, I had to take several breaths as the searing pain began. It was completely different from holding your baby and nursing. There must be an endorphin that kicks in to help with the pain. Thank God for endorphins; they are a wonderful part of our bodies.

I began talking to God again. I was begging and praying. "Please, God, let Ryken be okay. Please, God, let Ryken be okay." That was my mantra. The pain in my breasts subsided, but the pain in my chest grew.

That was my new routine every few hours besides keeping a bedside vigil with Ryken. I drank tons of water, swallowed my supplements, and ate healthy food in between pumping. I went into the special room to pump and pray. Ryken would need the breast milk. It was the nourishment his body needed to grow big and strong. As I pumped, I closed my eyes and prayed. I repeated my mantras for Ryken and his healing. The day ended with Brett going to his brother's house to sleep.

I went back to my room to sleep around ten. Another mom and her baby were on the other side of the curtain. I tried not to feel envious or jealous at their good fortunate. I brushed my teeth, got into bed and closed my eyes.

Tomorrow would be my birthday. I said a silent wish for myself: "Let Ryken be okay. Good night, Brett, Kaden, and Ryken. I love each of you."

I wake up in the middle of the night and walk down the long hallway to NICU to pump again. I stop to kiss my baby before I pumped. He is sleeping though and I do not want to wake him. Instead of touching him I tell him telepathically that I love him and reassure him that he would be okay soon as I gaze down at this precious child of mine.

I go and pump, saying my prayers over and over again. After I stored my breast milk in the freezer, as I do not know at this point when Ryken will need it. I walk over to say good night to my handsome boy.

He lays there beautiful and quiet amid the buzzing of the neonatal sounds. I leaned down and caressed my baby's hand, unable to hold myself back from touching him. "See you in the morning, Ryken. Sweet dreams. I love you."

I padded softly to my room and got under the covers. I would sleep for a few hours and repeat the process again in the morning. Brett would be here soon and Kaden was visiting sometime today. I fell asleep instantly.

I woke up somewhat refreshed after three hours. *My best birthday gift ever is down the hall. Today is my thirty-first birthday.*

I entered NICU, washed my hands, and kissed my baby. The nurses were busy as ever, and the sun was shining through the windows. I pumped and prayed, and returned to Ryken's bedside. Brett was there waiting for me. He gave me a hug and kiss and said happy birthday. We hugged each other and watched over our new gift lying before us. Within a few minutes we headed back to my room for breakfast during the doctors' rounds since parents were not allowed in NICU at that time due to confidentiality of the babies.

We returned to Ryken's bedside just after nine, and a social worker let us know she was there to help. She asked if we had any questions. I had worked with her on a professional level, and it was nice to see a familiar face. At this time we had no questions but it was nice to know we had someone to talk to if the need arose.

The doctor told us that Ryken would be given a CAT scan of his brain. They would also keep Ryken heavily sedated and maintain the dose of anti-seizure medication.

Ryken was taken down for the scan, and we were unable to go with him. We went to the cafeteria and found something that was packed with nutrition for a nursing mom. We hastily ate and walked back to NICU. Each of us wondered what the scan would show.

At 10:40 am we went over to Ryken's bedside. The details were relayed to us. The lab technician took Ryken's blood for a routine test. As soon as the blood work was complete, Ryken had begun desaturating to 65 percent for his oxygen-intake levels. More oxygen was given, and they used a special bag over his face to bring up his oxygen levels.

As soon as we were notified, Ryken began to have a seizure. He was desaturating to 48 percent. Ryken's face turned blue, his eyes became fixed and dilated, and his body stiffened. His jaw clenched, and his tongue was on the roof of his mouth. They used the same oxygen procedure of "bagging him".

Ryken was still having difficulty breathing. His saturation was 96 percent now though. Ryken was still having trouble breathing on his own. He finally gasped for air and was breathing again.

Ryken was transferred to the intensive care side of the unit. My anxiety and fear grew, and I pushed them away. I told myself it was going to be okay. *This is just a side effect from the brain swelling.*

Once he was moved and settled, we met his new nurse. Every day, there was a different nurse for the babies, and we didn't get to know the nurses that well before a new one appeared. I was sure it was to help the nurses maintain their efficiency and their sanity. I watched how wonderful and competent they were with my baby. I was very thankful for each of them. They had amazing hearts, and I said a silent prayer for the medical staff that was helping Ryken.

We spoke with another NICU doctor. Three of them worked there on a rotational shift. We had been talking with each of them, depending on who was on duty. Ryken had numerous episodes throughout the night with apnea. His breathing slowed down, and the oxygen levels in his blood decreased, which they referred to as desaturation. He was also twitching. They observed some seizure activity as well. The doctors thought it was still due to brain swelling.

A sling held his left arm in place, and a splint was applied with a cloth diaper to aid in his immobilization. Ryken's eyes and ears were covered. He was sucking on a soother. I felt it was a good sign that he was able to self-soothe.

At noon, Ryken was settled and quiet. There was no seizure activity, and we went down to the cafeteria for lunch. At one thirty, Ryken was given another EEG test.

At two thirty, Ryken was doing well. His vitals were stable. He was awake for small periods and was sucking on his soother eagerly. He even smiled occasionally. His left arm was immobilized again, and there was good blood flow to his fingers.

At five o'clock, I went to pump. Brett remained with Ryken. Ryken was still settled and sucking on his soother. He was given antibiotics to ensure there was no infection that his body was battling. There was no seizure activity at this time either.

I was pumping and saying my prayers. Ryken was doing well for several hours. Thank you, God. I was so happy and excited. I went back to the bedside, and Brett and I left to eat supper in the cafeteria since Ryken was doing so well. We headed down at five thirty for my birthday supper. I was mindful to continue to eat well and drink water to produce my breast milk. I was thrilled and happy that Ryken was doing so much better. We ordered and ate quickly. I was grateful that we could grab something to eat at the hospital and that we did not have to leave the NIC unit for long.

At six o'clock, we entered the ward and washed our hands. We glanced over to Ryken's bassinet and saw there was a team at his bedside. Many of the individuals were wearing blue scrubs. They had an airbag over Ryken's face. He had stopped breathing and was starting to convulse and seizure. He had become rigid, and his arms and legs were twitching. He had just been given his maintenance anti-seizure medication. The head doctor gave permission for another dose of phenobarbital.

Brett and I watched in horror and moved away while the medical team worked to help our baby. We were told they had called in the respiratory team. Ryken needed to be intubated for his breathing. They asked us to sign a consent form. We signed our names immediately.

Ryken was beginning to relax, but he stopped breathing again. His body became stiff and he was arching. His chest wall was rigid, and the team continued to bag his face. They attempted to intubate Ryken, but the tube was not in the right position. The second attempt to intubate was unsuccessful as well.

After the third try, they were finally successful. They put a flexible tube into his lungs. Ryken was on a machine that would help him breathe. He was still desaturating to 60 percent and then below 30 percent. His body was stiffening, and his chest wall was rigid. With the bagging, the tube was dislodged.

There was a fourth re-intubation attempt with the air bagging. Ryken's saturation dropped below 40 percent, and they discontinued the intubation process. More phenobarbital was given. Ryken has relaxed, his saturation level was 99 percent, and his heart rate was 144. They were trying to intubate him for the fifth time. Finally, Ryken relaxed.

He was also bagged again, and his saturation was 99 percent. He was having good chest expansion, and his coloring was pink.

Ryken was given Ativan to produce a calming effect on the central nervous system. He was given additional phenobarbital to reduce and stop the seizures.

The doctor informed us that he wanted to do a lumbar puncture for more testing. We signed papers giving our permission. At this point we would sign anything in order to save Ryken. He was moved to the most intensive care part of NICU, which was at the very front. We met our new nurse. Ryken appeared to be settled and had a bit of jaundice now. His left arm was propped up with a sling to help his collarbone continue to heal.

Brett looked into my eyes and said, "Pam, what is going on?" I could hear the helpless frustration in his voice.

I looked at Brett. There were tears in his eyes. For once in my life, no words would come. I said, "I don't know." I could only hug him as the tears streamed down my face. There were no words to ease Brett's pain and fears. It was the most helpless moment I had ever shared with another human being.

We were clinging to each other in the middle of NICU, drowning in our own pain and fear of the unknown. We clung to each other like a person would cling to a lifesaving device. The only problem was that we were floating and safe, but our baby wasn't. We could not find a lifesaving device for Ryken. The pain and helplessness were beyond measure.

We were notified after Ryken was stabilized and the intubation procedure was completed. The doctor ordered metabolic testing to be done since there was a concern that Ryken's issues were possibly due to a metabolic condition.

We needed to sign papers for the spinal tap. They would take out some of Ryken's cerebrospinal fluid (CSF). CSF is a clear fluid found in the brain and the spine, which is made in the choroid plexus of the brain. The plan for Ryken was to begin the metabolic testing to find out if that was the underlying cause of his issues. It was also decided he would be given a different round of antibiotics to rule out any infections.

I will never forget this birthday. In my mind, branded to my brain, was the picture of everyone around Ryken. They were working so hard to try to save his life. Nothing in my life that I have dealt with had been as painful as watching a group of people try and save my baby's life.

Brett left the hospital at ten o'clock to get some sleep at his brother's house. I returned to my room and got ready for bed. I was the only mom in there, and I didn't have to make any small talk. I had been discharged from the hospital, but I was able to pay ten dollars a day to stay in the room. Thank God for that room.

I set my alarm to pump during the night. I said good night to my boys and asked God to take care of Ryken. I was able to close my eyes and drift into sleep. My whole world was upside down. There were no answers about Ryken. All I knew for sure was that every day seemed worse than the previous one.

The following morning, October 21, we spent the day in NICU. At nine o'clock, we arrived at Ryken's bedside. The nurse notified us that we were allowed to touch Ryken, but it has to be a "solid touch." We were not allowed to stroke his arm or rub his skin.

Ryken was having some "normal" activity when the nurse did his mouth care and opened his eyes. Ryken was moving his left arm on his own. The nurse noted that the flow of blood to Ryken's fingers was good. That was a great sign that his collarbone was healing. We remained there for the day and quietly talked to Ryken. We whispered words of healing and hope into our sweet baby's ears. We coaxed our "champion" along.

Ryken had been convulsing for about two hours that morning. He only responded to massive doses of phenobarbital that were used to control and reduce Ryken's seizures. They began the metabolic workup; the doctor performed the spinal tap and sent the fluid away for metabolic testing. No results would be known for at least a week as the samples had to be shipped out for testing.

When Ryken convulsed, all of his extremities would stiffen. The tonic-clonic seizures were generalized seizures that affected the entire brain. They are also known as grand mal seizures that are often associated with epilepsy. Ryken would go completely rigid. He was also fighting to breathe and had periods of apnea when his breathing would slow or stop. It was a godsend when he was ventilated.

The plan for Ryken was to keep him sedated while maintaining his phenobarbital medication. We needed to have patience. It would be a long wait. It would take a long time to see if the metabolic testing would be a helpful piece of the puzzle. There might be answers hidden in Ryken's cerebrospinal fluid.

On October 23, Ryken had an electroencephalogram (EEG). The test shows the type and location of activities in the brain during seizures. The procedure tracks and records brain patterns. It also provides evidence of how the brain functions over time. Ryken's results from the EEG testing showed signs of seizure activity and burst-suppression patterns.

We developed a routine. Kaden was brought for brief visits every other day. We would meet in the sitting area outside of the neonatal unit. He was doing well and thriving with his grandparents. I had enough to worry about with Ryken. The grandparents would visit Ryken while we had some time with Kaden. Sometimes we would go down to the cafeteria with him. I missed him and felt the weight a mother feels when she has to be with one child but is carrying guilt for being away from the other one. It was difficult being a parent. Everything was easy when I lived in the land of ignorance.

On October 24, Ryken had swelling around his eyes, arms, legs, feet, and scrotum. The nurse noted that Ryken was having some jerky movements when he was handled and when he was undisturbed in the bassinet. Due to the intubation, there were a lot of thick and frothy secretions in Ryken's mouth. The nurse suctioned Ryken's mouth to remove a large amount of the secretions. There was a large air leak, and the respiratory team was notified.

Today was a happy day. Ryken was given the expressed breast milk I had pumped through a gavage tube that ran from his mouth to his stomach. He was given twenty milliliters every three or four hours. Ryken had not been given any breast milk since October 19. I was so excited that he was finally able to take some of the breast milk. It was encouraging news for us.

Blood work was done again, and Ryken was given another CAT scan. It showed that he still had some brain swelling in the white matter of his brain. There was a suggestion that it may be due to epilepticus seizure activity. We were asked about epilepsy in our family histories. Brett's paternal grandmother and paternal aunt had the condition, but there was no one else that we were aware of.

Ryken had no convulsions since he was intubated that day. The antibiotics were discontinued when the cultures came back negative to any kind of infections in his body.

On October 25, Ryken was quiet and helpless as he lay in his little bassinet. We were allowed to touch him, change his diaper, and wipe his lips. We were also allowed to apply Vaseline to his dry lips to bring back some hydration and softness to them.

Ryken had been given intravenous, and they began to increase the amount of expressed breast milk he was given. I was so glad that I had been pumping diligently. They were giving Ryken the breast milk through an oral gastric tube, which was a step in the right direction. We were working toward recovery, and he was getting some nutrition. It was very exciting for us. It was making pumping and praying a lot easier.

On October 26, our baby was eight days old. Ryken's feedings were increased, which was great news. There had been no seizure activity. I had a routine of pumping every two or three hours, drinking a ton of water, and eating as healthily as I could. I also took my supplements religiously.

I was at Ryken's bedside at every possible moment. I stroked his arm and held his little hand. Brett was working on a crossword puzzle. We were both feeling better and more optimistic.

Another test that was performed on Ryken was an echocardiogram, which showed evidence of a small perimembranous ventricular septal defect. It was a defect in the ventricular septum (the wall dividing the left and right ventricles of the heart). I got a feeling from the doctors that it seemed to be less of an issue for Ryken at this time.

CHAPTER 10

Judgment Day

On October 28, I walked down to neonatal after I gulped down my breakfast. I headed over to see Ryken and asked the nurse how the past few hours had been for him. Ryken was doing about the same, and no concerns were noted. Brett showed up after I pumped, and we spent time with Ryken at his bedside.

Ryken had been given twenty milliliters of my breast milk through a gavage tube. I was hopeful that the nutrition would make him stronger. I told myself we were on the mend—and that it was a good sign. He could grow with the nutrition he was getting because he was ten days old today.

We were notified that the head of neurology for pediatrics had come in from another city to assess Ryken and look over his case. There was a meeting set up for us with Dr. Dowry at one o'clock.

We went about our morning routine taking care of Ryken with the nurse, and kept a bedside vigil with him. I did my pumping and praying. Brett and I went to the cafeteria for an early lunch since we did not want to be late for our appointment. I was looking forward to the meeting with the doctors.

Ryken was doing so much better. I wondered what they would tell us about the brain swelling. Ryken's brain should have been completely normal by then, especially with how well he was doing. There should be no more swelling of his brain was my thought. I had butterflies in my tummy as I ate. I was so excited to finally hear some good news.

We headed back up to the second floor in the elevator. We walked down the hall to the offices just outside of neonatal. I took a breath and knocked. The door opened, and we were invited in. As we stepped into the doctor's office, the introductions were made. Brett and I sat together on the loveseat.

Both doctors were behind the desk. They took turns speaking to us. "We have a diagnosis. The baby's glycine levels were elevated. Dr. Dowry, the pediatric neurologist, monitored him last night. He observed that the baby's arms were jerking, his tongue was moving, and his knees were drawn up."

This is nothing new except they possibly know what is wrong. I made myself focus on their faces.

"An EEG was repeated to assess the burst-suppression pattern in Ryken's brain since birth. The EEG was worsening, so the outcome is the probability of more severe seizures. The diagnosis we have is called nonketotic hyperglycinemia."

I was listening intently. I had no idea what Brett was thinking. My gaze was fixated on the doctors. As I listened, coldness gripped my body, and I shivered even though the temperature in the room was the same.

"There is no treatment for this condition. Ryken's convulsions will continue. This is part of the condition. There is a chance of this condition reoccurring in a subsequent pregnancy. The statistics are one out of four pregnancies, which means there is a 25 percent chance in each pregnancy that the baby will have this condition."

I was shaking inside, trembling from the truth that resonated in each syllable that was uttered to me. In every word that was relayed to us, my body was fighting against a frost that I could not escape. The cold was trying to settle in my heart. I would not allow it in.

"Each of you are a carrier of this condition in order for the baby to have it."

This makes no sense to me. Brett and I are carriers of this condition? We did this to Ryken? How could this have happened?

Thankfully, my body provided a blanket of shock so I could cover up with it and keep my heart warm. I continued to listen.

The room began to feel hot and spacey. Reality settled in, but it was intermingled with numbness, disbelief, and a searing pain inside my heart. It was unbearable. I thanked God for these emotions because they allowed my brain to find the words to form a sentence.

I looked the doctors in the eye and said, "Are you telling me that my baby is going to die?"

I heard the answer to the question that I dared to ask. I so desperately needed an answer to the question, but I did not want to hear it.

The doctors look at me. The specialist said, "Yes."

My brain was on overload. My world started to spin and became very small.

That is not the word I expected. That is not the word I wanted to hear.

I asked, "How long will he live?" I did not recognize my own voice. I was on autopilot. I was a zombie held captive within my own body. The magnitude of the truth that has just been spoken was too much for me to internalize. The truth was too difficult to comprehend.

Dr. Dowry said, "I have only worked with one other case of a baby who had NKH, and that baby lived for six months. That baby was given sodium benzoate. It is a medicine that helps to bring the glycine levels down in the body."

What is glycine—and NKH and will sodium benzoate help Ryken?

It would not allow him to live forever. I heard the words "six months" again.

I felt as if we were trapped in the dark. The darkness that had fallen on our lives left no shadow or way to find the light. The light was no longer ours.

Brett and I listened in painful silence. We only had six months left with Ryken. That was a guess if compared to another baby who had the same condition. *This NKH, nonketotic hyperglycinemia condition that my beautiful baby has just been diagnosed with.* If Ryken was barely two weeks old, we only had five and a half months left with him.

The walls were closing in around me, and I felt myself shutting down. The words I had heard left me immobilized. It was hard to breathe. I tried to maintain my focus. I felt like passing out, but I knew that I couldn't. I wanted to scream, but my voice didn't work. I wanted to shout out to them that they were wrong, but I didn't. My vocal cords had been tied in knots. The only thing they were capable of right then was stillness. I tried to focus on my breathing.

I wanted to hit something, but I kept my hands folded neatly in my lap. I wanted to ask God what we ever did to deserve this. I held my tongue. I remained silent.

I wanted to scream at the doctors to fix it. Instead, I looked at them quietly. I didn't like them even though they hadn't done anything. That was not true. I didn't even know them. I had nothing against them except that I didn't like the news they had given me. Would the truth set us free?

In our case, the truth left me shackled to a condition called nonketotic hyperglycinemia. We would never be free again. I couldn't even pronounce or spell the truth. This truth was written in our DNA, and now it was written in Ryken's.

The truth was Ryken's death sentence. Our genes collided because of our desire for another child. *We did this to Ryken.*

As the seconds slowly crept by, I heard the clock on the wall ticking. With each passing moment, my heart broke into tiny, shattered pieces. I was unable to keep the frost at bay as it engulfed my heart.

Words are powerful. They can be powerful enough to instill a ray of hope inside you or move mountains. They can be powerful enough to break your heart or shatter your dreams. The words we heard did the latter. I was expecting to jump on the ray of hope and ride it into the sunset when I left this room after our meeting.

Instead, the words left me breathless. I was unable to take a deep breath or speak. By breathing, you are living. I was breathing, which meant I was living. I was living, which meant I had to face reality. I had to face the truth.

The reality that they had bestowed upon us was that they had no lifesaving device for Ryken. They were going to stand on the shore and watch Ryken slowly drown. Before the meeting, Brett and I were hopeful that the two doctors would help us, and save our baby. We thought they would provide us with the best lifesaving device we could imagine. The reality—the truth—was that they wouldn't. Not because they didn't want to. The reality—the truth— was because they couldn't. I would despise having to tell parents that their babies are going to die.

I didn't care about them though. I was seething. The words that moved and swayed in my head were not kind. They were just there and they were not directed at anyone in particular. The feelings that moved through my body were not nice: rage, anguish, sadness, betrayal, hurt, pain, dread, shock, and denial. The smorgasbord of feelings was like nothing I had ever felt before. An indescribable helplessness was born from the truth. That was my new reality.

I was falling into a black pit of despair, and no one would reach out a hand to catch me and stop the fall. They just stared at me and watched as I fell deeper into the pit of unending pain and heartache.

With no words left to say, we left the doctor's office. Our first thought was Ryken, and we walked the fifty steps to see our baby.

With the news about his condition on my mind, I peered down at this treasure in front of me. Ryken looked like an angel as he slept. Soon he would become an angel.

His nurse asked us if we wanted to hold Ryken. I could see in her eyes that she knew our new reality. The nurse allowed us to hold him in the rocking chair beside his bassinet. Brett and I took turns holding our beautiful baby boy. We were very careful with all the cords and tubing attached to him. The machines were helping Ryken breathe and stay alive.

The air was thick with raw emotion, and there were no words that would make it evaporate. The rays of hope that had once danced playfully around Ryken's bassinet had stepped back to allow the impending rays of death to step forward and claim that space. Hope vanished, and doom had taken its place.

Brett gently passed Ryken over for my turn with him. I settled in the rocker and looked down at Ryken. He was sleeping peacefully. Tears streamed down my face, but I did not care. I snuggled him as gently as I could—even though I wanted to hug him tightly to my broken heart. I never wanted to let him go. I never wanted to face the words I had just heard.

I wanted to wake up from that nightmare and pretend it was only a dream—a crazy dream that we could laugh at. I could take comfort from our family and friends as they reassured me that babies don't die in real life. In real life, my baby did not have any kind of condition. In real life, my baby was healthy and thriving. I would watch him grow up with Kaden. I would see him play hockey and fight with his big brother.

I looked into Ryken's face. My little "Champion" was so precious and special. I rocked him and wept. I wept about the news that I only had five and a half months left with him. I wept with the reality that maybe I did not even have that long. I wept with the pain of a mother who could not do anything to help her child. Praying had done nothing. God had ignored me. I felt the anger rising within me. I was so sad that the anger would not win right then. Despair was the winning emotion that claimed the space in my mind and body.

After a few moments, I passed Ryken over to Brett. I was trying to be mindful to share him. I saw the pain in Brett's eyes. I was overcome with the awful, cruel news. *What about all my prayers to God when I pumped and prayed? I asked God for a miracle? This is not a miracle. This is a cruel twist of fate. I can't believe this is happening to us.*

The social worker came over to talk to us. In a way, it was nice to see a familiar face. However, I did not want to see anyone I knew: acquaintance, family member, or friend. For a moment, I wondered if it was more difficult for her since she knew me.

She told us she was sorry to hear our news. Her advice was to keep a journal and write everything down in it. She would be there to help us, and she left her card if we needed to contact her for anything. We thanked her, and she left.

When will I have time write in a journal? How am I supposed to do that? All I wanted to do was hold Ryken before he died. I cried again silently.

My mind moved forward to the next thought. I was thankful that Kaden was on his way to the hospital. I wanted a family picture. I needed a family picture before it was too late—before Ryken was gone.

CHAPTER 11

First Family Picture

Kaden arrived with my mom and stepdad. I hugged him and held on to him for dear life. I kissed his cheeks and stroked his hair. I felt the energy in his body and his breath on my face. I was thankful and grateful that he was born without NKH. That condition that had claimed Ryken as it's own.

We told my parents the news, but I was having difficulty fathoming it. I saw the pain in their eyes and the shock on their faces as I relayed to them what we had just been told. They were speechless. It was a lot to take in, and I found it difficult to comprehend what I had just told them.

Seeing their faces was hurtful, but it was nothing like the pain in my heart. My chest was on fire. I was unable to scream—even though that was all I wanted to do. I wanted to swear at the world and lash out at God. I kept those thoughts and feelings to myself. I stuffed down the anger. I swallowed the pain and emotions as best as I could. I pushed it further away and down into the pit of pain below. It was gurgling and bubbling somewhere down there, threatening to explode at any moment.

Time was of the essence so we got our first family pictures. Brett, Kaden, Ryken, and I sat together in the neonatal unit. Within the hour of hearing that Ryken would die, we were posing together and trying to smile. They made an exception and allowed Kaden into NICU to see his brother and take the pictures.

I was smiling like a fool with red eyes from crying for the past hour. I felt like it was our one and only chance at a family picture. I was smiling out of happiness that we would have a family picture—the four of us together as I had dreamed about. There were no pictures of us as a family yet. To me, it was a treasured gift and possibly a rare moment in time for the four of us.

I looked at my husband and felt so much sadness. Brett could barely smile for the camera. His hand rested on his throat as though it could cover up the big lump of pain sitting there. His eyes said it all. There was a heart so broken, and there was nothing to fix it. There was no twinkle and no light left in my husband's eyes.

Nothing would fix Ryken and make it better. I was unable to help him. Our second son who looked identical to his father was going to die because we passed on a rare genetic condition to him. It happened unknowingly, but that does not change anything or lessen the pain.

We gave Ryken back to the nurse so he could rest in his bassinet. We were shown to a small room just outside of NICU where we could make our phone calls in private. We contacted the rest of our parents and siblings. Finding the words to tell them was hard. I told them what we had been told. I spoke, but it did not sound like me. My voice sounded odd, and my throat was aching with pain. The lump in my throat was making it hard to say the words that had to be spoken. Time was ticking way. I said, "We have been given bad news today. Ryken has a rare genetic condition called nonketotic hyperglycinemia. Brett and I are carriers. He is not going to live. We are unsure how long he will be here. The doctors don't know. If you would like to see him, you should come soon. You should come today."

I got the words out, but the burning tears in my eyes were hard to control. They were trying to burst forth like a dam of water, bursting at the edges. They wanted to rush forth and wreak havoc on everything in its path. Inside I wanted to lash out at something. I keep the rage at bay—for the moment.

Instead, I made myself focus and listen to the other person on the other end of the phone.

"It would have been nice to know about this condition before you and Brett got married."

I heard that statement, but I didn't give it much thought. I was not angry at the response or the person. Sometimes when we hear something that is so unbelievable, we go into shock. The filters in our brains stop working. Some things were said that might not have seemed appropriate at the time, but I was not offended. I had bigger things to take up my emotions.

We were all processing the news in our own ways. I loved Brett, and I wanted to marry him. We wanted to have our own family together. It all sounded so simple and easy. It *was* so simple and easy until now.

I was in no frame of mind to chat about whether I should have married Brett or not because we are now carriers of a rare genetic condition. I was barely coping. I had more calls to make, and I wanted to go back to the neonatal unit to hold Ryken.

I had to call one of my sisters at her place of employment. She told her coworker why she had to leave immediately for the hospital. Word got out that the Larocque baby was dying. In a small community like ours, that kind of news spreads like wildfire. Thirsty plants in the desert were burning with the news and lighting up the sky as it traveled around. Flames were licking their way from mouth to mouth as people talked.

Our world was turned upside down, and people in the real world were chatting about my life. It was out of my control, and some people heard the news through the grapevine. There were hurt feelings because the news did not come directly from us. I guess people are allowed to own their feelings. I was only going to worry about what was in my control. At the moment I was slowly losing control of my life as I was going to lose my baby to NKH. My plate was full. The Serenity Prayer helped me through many obstacles in life. "God, grant me the serenity to accept the things I cannot change, the courage to change the things I can, and the wisdom to know the difference."

I felt the rage of anger in me trying to make its way up to express itself. It was as if someone threw a lit match on gas-soaked wood in the fire pit of rage that was already going on deep within myself. I repeated the prayer several times in my mind and felt myself feeling better.

When a person speaks out of anger, it can be harmful. A fire destroys everything in its path, leaving nothing but a mess of charred blackness that is good for nothing and no one. That was how words can leave a person feeling if spoken by someone in a rage of anger. I tried to calm down before talking to anyone.

I was trying to cope the best I could with the news that my baby was going to die. On my to-do list was calling our parents and siblings to tell them the news. I could barely speak to my immediate family because of my pain. I had no time to talk to anyone else.

I felt myself getting more anxious by the minute. Each minute I spent on the phone was one minute less with Ryken. I was also carrying guilt about Kaden and not seeing very much of him these past ten days.

I had no time for other people's hurt feelings. I let it go and allowed them to own them. I knew the phone calls our family received from us sent them into their own states of shock, numbness, helplessness, and hopelessness. Those emotions were running through everyone.

Our last phone call was complete and we went back to be by Ryken's side. We were approached by the doctor and told that Ryken's glycine levels were not typical with the levels they should see for a baby with nonketotic hyperglycinemia. His levels should have been much higher if he had NKH. The doctor wanted to do another lumbar puncture on Ryken.

What do we say to this? Do we say no? Is there a chance the diagnosis is wrong?

We signed more papers and gave our consent.

Is that a flicker of light I see in the corner of the darkened room we live in now? Is there hope again?

CHAPTER 12

Last Resort

I had the distinct urge to contact the healers who had helped me along my path. I told Brett that I would leave no stone unturned to help Ryken. If the doctors were telling us there was nothing they could do, I wanted to see who else could help him. I needed to do it, and Brett agreed with me. I hoped they could help Ryken.

With what little hope I had left, I notified the doctors that I would be bringing in a person who did energy work and reflexology. The doctors did not say no. The way I spoke to them and the way I looked them directly in the eye left no room for them to say no to me. If I had been in their position, I would not have had the heart to say no to me either.

I contacted the healer that evening and explained Ryken's prognosis. Brita agreed to come the following afternoon at one o'clock to give Ryken a treatment. It would be twenty-four hours after we were given the devastating news.

I felt a surge of hope in my heart. This woman had helped me when I was sick. Her daughter had gotten me on the right track when I had iron poisoning. The women in that family had a gift from God. I was not ashamed to reach out and beg for help for Ryken.

What wouldn't I do for him? I am looking for a miracle, and miracles happen every day to normal people. Why not us? We are normal. Aren't we? To a certain degree, we are. I don't feel normal anymore. Maybe I'm not normal. Regardless I am his mother and my job is to do whatever I can for Ryken.

I was counting on Brita and God to help Ryken. I was putting all my eggs in their basket. I was praying that she would have the miracle I had been waiting for. Time was ticking by slowly but surely for Ryken. I tried not to panic or think about him dying.

It was almost nine o'clock when my sisters entered NICU. They had come to see Ryken. We were given special permission, and they were allowed to come in and meet him. I believe in rules and following them. I also believe there are times to bend them in certain circumstances. This was one of those times. They had only seen Ryken through the glass window, but now they could actually touch his skin and see the wonder that is Ryken.

We walked over to Ryken's bassinet. A strong sense of pride filled my heart as I showed off my sweet baby to my little sisters, his Aunty Deann and Aunty Mindy. It was a moment of joy and sorrow for me. Both emotions intertwined in a twisted knot held captive within my heart.

We stood together for a few moments, and they softly touched Ryken's hands.

Deann softly speaks, "He looks too strong and healthy to be so sick. He looks out of place in here."

I would have agreed, but there was no denying what we had been told earlier that day.

The tears that fell from our eyes were the only form of communication that was needed. There were no words to say that would help. After the short visit with him, we left NICU together, and my sisters hugged me good-bye. Neither of them was a mother yet, but they understood that today was the worst day of my life because Ryken's diagnosis of NKH could mean a death sentence for him.

I went to bed that night, grasping onto hope. I hoped that Brita was going to work her magic. I hoped that she would tell me something positive tomorrow afternoon. I set my alarm to wake me up so I could go and pump in a few hours. You never know and I was not giving up on Ryken yet.

Good night, my sweet boys. I love you. God help Ryken tomorrow. Please bless us with a miracle. Do you hear my prayers, God? I want a miracle tomorrow! Time will tell. I sure hate that saying.

Brita arrived at the hospital at one o'clock. We were watching for her outside of NICU. My heart filled with warmth, and it was beating so fast as I saw her. I quickly approached her and thanked her for coming to see Ryken.

We entered the ward and went through the protocol of washing our hands with her. We immediately went over to where our son lay. She began her touch therapy and placed her hands on Ryken. She began with his feet, the area above the liver, and the back of his neck. She told us that the medications were affecting his liver. She worked on that area to get Ryken's liver working properly again. She did the energy work for about twenty minutes. She instructed us to let him rest and recover. His body had been through a lot. She was in her seventies and had a no-nonsense air about her.

She agreed to come back the following day at one o'clock. I walked her out, thanking her as I hugged her good bye.

I returned to NICU and sat by Ryken's bedside with Brett. We watched our baby while the beeps and sounds of the NICU swirled around us.

I was beginning to feel small rays of hope. It was as though small beams of energy were sifting through the darkness and shedding light on our situation. Hope was a place I would like to be in, and I asked God to send me more. I thanked God for the gift of the healer who had helped Ryken today.

I was still pumping and eating the best I could to produce milk for my baby. Ryken would need the milk when he got better. The hours ticked by, and it was time to go to bed. I was still staying in the dormitory room for mothers.

Brett and I hugged good-bye. I held onto him for a moment longer, not wanting to let him go. We both needed sleep. Tomorrow would be another day, and we would need to be rested to deal with whatever came our way.

CHAPTER 13

Hope: Today Is Better than Yesterday

On October 30, I ate my breakfast, pumped my breast milk, and spent every spare moment with Ryken and Brett. I was anxiously awaiting Brita's arrival.

Brita arrived right on time, and I led her into NICU. She worked on Ryken for about fifteen minutes. She began at his feet and placed her hands over his liver and at his neck just like before. She told us to let him rest as much as possible so his body could heal. She planned to come back the next evening at six thirty.

The nurse asked us if we wanted to hold him, but we told her we would let him rest after his healing session. That was what Brita had instructed us to do. We continued with our bedside vigil. I continued to pray to God. I hoped he was listening to me. I had felt ignored by him lately. The afternoon ticked by, and Ryken continued to rest.

When it was time for bed, we left Ryken for the night. There were no changes in him; he was sleeping and still. I went to sleep in my dorm room. I was excited for his third treatment. *Good night, my sweet boys. Sweet dreams. I love you.*

The next day was Halloween. Kaden was at Brett's brother's home. We had not decided what we would do for Kaden today. He had his Tigger costume and was set if he went out for a few blocks of trick-or-treating with his aunt and uncle.

The day goes by and we kept up our bedside vigil with Ryken and sat quietly with him in NICU. That had become our new normal.

At 4:50, Ryken's ventilator began ringing, and there was tension noted on the endotracheal tube (ETT) that had been inserted through his mouth to his lungs. The nursing staff listened to the ETT, and it had become dislodged. They pulled it out. I guessed that Ryken and God felt it needed to come out. The doctors were notified, and two hours after being extubated, Ryken's vital signs were stable. Ryken was breathing on his own! I was so excited that I could have jumped up and down and screamed for joy. Instead, I smiled and whispered, "Ryken, you are a champion. Keep healing. I know you will get better." I thanked God silently in my head.

I could hardly believe what was going on, but it was an evening of pure rejoicing. Ryken had decided he no longer needed the ventilator. I knew that Brita's treatments were working and helping Ryken heal. I was able to gaze at my beautiful baby's face because it was free of the tubing. His skin was red and splotchy from the tape that was holding all the tubes in place. His skin would heal. That was the least of our concerns.

Ryken was trying to open his eyes. I peered down at my baby and we looked at each other. "There's those beautiful eyes Ryken. I have missed seeing them." My heart was about to burst and a smile spread across my face as I spoke to my baby.

Since he had been taken off the ventilator, we were beginning to feed him. He was tolerating his feedings well and was getting breast milk through a tube that ran down into his throat via his nose. I was feeling and seeing a miracle happen before my very eyes. I could hardly contain myself.

Brita came in for her third session with Ryken. I was happy about his progress, and I thanked her profusely for her help and the work she was doing for him. I was so happy that I had followed my gut instinct and contacted her. She was a kind and humble woman.

Brita worked on Ryken again and left after thirty minutes. She told us that he needed to rest after the healing session but was doing better.

The nurse noted some fine tremors, but there were no seizures. Our nurse was smiling at us, and we felt hope circulating around Ryken. We left him to rest. We knew how great he was doing. Since Ryken was doing so well, we decided we could spend a few hours with Kaden. It was Halloween, and we wanted to spend part of Halloween with him.

As we drove over to Brett's brother's house, it felt different to be outside of the hospital. The crisp autumn air and driving along the street felt like sensory overload after being inside the hospital for so long.

I was excited to see my little buddy. I had missed Kaden so much. We had been apart for fourteen days. I said a silent prayer and thanked our families for stepping up and taking care of our sunshine.

When we arrived, Kaden was carving a pumpkin in the kitchen with his grandma. He was having so much fun digging with his tiny hands and pulling out the guts of the pumpkin in earnest. We hugged him and squeezed him a bit harder than usual. It was a gift to have him in our lives. He was healthy and thriving.

We played for a little and enjoyed the short reprieve from the stress that surrounded us at the hospital. Kaden dressed up in his Tigger costume, and we went trick-or-treating for twenty minutes. I felt normal again for those brief moments. In the back of my mind, I knew Ryken needed me. I felt guilty for being there with Kaden. With my next breath, I felt guilty because Kaden needed me too. My emotions were so complicated. The one that I disliked the most was guilt.

We say good-bye to a content and happy boy. He was not crying that we were leaving, which was a blessing. He seemed to be adjusting to his new life of not knowing when he would see his parents next.

We headed back to the hospital, which was only a fifteen-minute drive. I prayed that Ryken was still doing well.

We arrived in NICU and quickly went to Ryken's bassinet. He was doing amazing. His nurse notified us that he had done well for the past several hours. I felt like my heart was going to burst with joy. I could see my beautiful baby's face, and he opened his eyes. I leaned down, looked into them, and felt a deep connection. Our souls said hello through our eyes. I spoke softly in a voice that was full of happiness.

There had been no tremors while we were away. There had also been no obvious seizures, and Ryken had not desaturated. He was given breast milk through an oral gastric tube. At his last feeding, the nurse had increased it by ten milliliters. He had been gaining weight. The air prongs were in his nose, and he looked so different now that we could see his face.

He was so cute and beautiful, and he was healing and thriving. His feedings were increasing slowly, and I was so happy he was able to get that breast milk I worked so diligently for. I kissed him, rubbed our noses together, and gave him Eskimo kisses. "Hello, Ryken. How's my big boy?" It was so different to hold him and not be fearful of hurting him because of the tubing in his lungs.

I was smiling from ear to ear. *Miracles do happen. I am witnessing one right now. Thank you, God. Thank you, Brita. Thank you, Ryken, for being such a fighter. You are my champion.*

I went to bed and prayed for the miracle to continue. I smiled myself to sleep. *I can't wait until tomorrow to see how much better Ryken will be doing.*

The morning brought more progress. Ryken's nasal cannula was removed, and his oxygen remained good. He was given ten milliliters of breast milk by bottle, and his eyes were focusing a bit better. The nurse noticed some tremors of his hands and feet.

As the day went on, the doctor decided that Ryken's nasal prongs should be placed back in his nose when he was being held and during his feedings. Since Ryken was not interested in nursing, I used a shield that went over my breast. That really helped since Ryken would nurse that way.

Whenever I saw the doctor, I would be smiling. I would tell him how well Ryken was doing and how happy I was with his progress.

The doctor would look at me and say, "You know that he still has NKH, right? You know that he is still going to die?"

I would have no answer for those questions. I was unable to speak. It was like I was an excited child at a birthday party who was waiting to talk to the clown. As I approached him, he would turn to me and pop the balloon I was holding with his needle. Just like that, he would burst my bubble of hope with his words. I did not understand that he was trying to help me stay rooted in the reality of the situation.

I would vent to Brett after these conversations. I would say, "He just wants to burst my bubble. He is not looking at how well Ryken is doing." I was unable to see how his words were meant to help me. I felt like he was pulling the rug out from under me. He would place me back in reality, and I was fighting so hard to run away from it. The inevitable doom was chasing me and trying to get my baby. I would not let go of Ryken without a fight.

I chose to run full force down a side street called hope. I was darting and dashing away from the shadow of death that was chasing us. I really felt that we had escaped it, and a second chance was on the horizon. I guess it was our third chance if I count our Trisomy 18 scare. Ryken was doing well and getting better. I just needed the doctor to see it too.

I would not let anyone tell me differently as long as Ryken was improving. With every last breath, my plan was to ride the waves of optimism for as long as I could— hopefully forever. My waves were gaining ground, and I had no fear of crashing anytime soon.

The consensus was that Ryken was a mystery and that his improvements were baffling. He was our miracle baby. I continued swimming in the sea of prayers and hopefulness. Even some nurses were curious about our healer and what she did for Ryken since he was improving after each session.

Soon, Ryken was able to nurse completely free of a breast shield and without having to be topped up with the gavache tube. The nurses taught me how to administer Ryken's medications with a bottle. The sodium benzoate would bring down Ryken's glycine levels. The concern about the medication was that it could loosen his stools or give him diarrhea.

There was a certain protocol to the medication regime to minimize Ryken's side effects. It had to be taken with food, and certain medications had to be given first to counter the side effects of the sodium benzoate. Ryken was also on an anti-seizure medication.

On November 3, Ryken had no seizures. A decision was made to send him home in the near future. He was breast-feeding on demand, eating well, and gaining weight. I felt as though my miracle was happening. All my prayers were being answered.

On November 4, I met with the pharmacist to chat about the different medicines. Ryken was tolerating them so far, and there were no concerns yet. I felt joyful as I gave Ryken his medications in a bottle, nursed him, and held him again. My world had been put back in place, and I was full of hope.

By November 5, Ryken was exclusively getting all of his feedings from breast-feeding. His cries were lusty. My beautiful boy was making eye contact and had no seizures. I was grateful that the medications were helping him.

The following day was full of nothing but wonderful news. Ryken appeared to be tolerating his new medicine well. He continued to breast-feed and was gaining weight daily. Brett and I rocked him between his feedings, trying to make up for all the time he was alone in the bassinet. We were so happy and relieved. What a roller coaster ride it had been!

There was talk about being discharged the next day. I could not believe my ears. I was thrilled. Brett decided to go back to work the next day. My mom would spend the day with me and help me take Ryken home. Kaden was in good hands at our house with Brett's parents. Our world was wonderful again.

On November 7, I packed the few belongings in my dorm room and got ready to leave the place I had called home for the past twenty days. My mom and I took turns holding Ryken while the hospital got everything ready for his release.

That afternoon, I dressed Ryken in his "coming home" outfit. It took all day to get the medications sorted out so I could administer them at home. We were given the discharge papers and the plans for different doctor appointments over the next few months. I made sure all the paperwork and medications were packed safely in my diaper bag.

I looked down at my little miracle and love burst through my heart. Joy seeped out every pore as I packed up to leave NICU. I was grateful to every single staff member that helped play a role in Ryken's recovery. There were many faces I would never forget. I was so excited to be going home. I couldn't wait!

I was smiling and so full of joy. I couldn't believe it was really happening. We were going home! They gave us a certificate: "Congratulations! This was to certify that Ryken Larocque has successfully completed a course in NICU of twenty days and was one of our distinguished graduates. Graduation day: November 7, 2005." Hooray! I was so excited. It was Ryken's first diploma.

I was thankful to have my mom with me to celebrate that big step. Brett was at work for the first time in more than three weeks. I was beyond grateful to his employers for their generosity and kindness during our difficult time. I needed Brett with Ryken and me everyday. His supervisors had allowed Brett to focus on his family. I will always remember that gesture of humanity toward our family.

At six o'clock, we were released. Like birds, we flew the coop as quickly as we could. I put Ryken in a warm bunting bag and placed him in his car seat. I completed the five-point harness clips and tucked a blanket around his little body. It was chilly, but I did not care. The forty-five-minute drive was blissful. I sat in the back, watched Ryken sleep peacefully, and chatted with my mom. He was finally going home!

Brett, his parents, and Kaden greeted us at the door. I grabbed "Kadey Cocoa Puffs" in a bear hug and held him tightly. I did not want to let him go, and I took a deep breath of relief. I had missed him so much. I couldn't believe he was there too. We were together.

I could feel love swelling in my heart. I had forgotten what joy and peace felt like as well. I could not believe the day had come, but we were together. Dreams do come true. Thank you, God!

We took some happy homecoming pictures with everyone. We all had a bright light in our eyes. We celebrated the miracle of Ryken. It was the best picture yet! Happiness radiated from our smiles. We took our second official family picture at home with ease and grace. Nineteen days after Ryken's birth, we were home together. We were smiling in the picture like the family we were supposed to be. Brett and I were together with our two beautiful boys. I would sleep well tonight.

My mom decided to stay and help me for a few days. The following day, the health nurse came over to weigh Ryken and check on us. Ryken was gaining weight and nursing like a pro. I was feeling well and showing no signs of postpartum depression. Everything was going as planned. PPD must not have thought to look in NICU for me. Actually, maybe it knew I was there and gave me a break.

My anxiety was gone. I was surprised since there was a lot to do with the medications for Ryken. I had a list of when I needed to give him the medications and the feedings. I was coping well. Writing everything down was helpful, and there was no confusion that way.

Ryken was a content baby. He only cried when he was hungry, and he slept a lot. When he was awake, I rocked and snuggled with him.

When he was sleeping, Kaden peeked into the bassinet.

I asked, "What are you doing, Kaden?"

He replied, "Peeking at baby Ryken. Love him." I looked at Kaden in wonder and was happy he had his parents and baby home with him finally. It must have been a confusing time for our toddler.

I was so lucky to have my boys together. The thoughts and dreams I had during my pregnancy were coming true. I was feeling so calm and relaxed. My life was pure bliss again.

The boys and I got into a routine. Kaden still napped each afternoon for two or three hours, which allowed me to rest. Ryken also seemed to nap exactly when Kaden did as well. My boys are so good to their mom. Ryken woke up a few times at night to nurse even though I made sure he ate every two or three hours during the days.

The week went so well that we decided to visit Brett's parents for the day. They lived ninety minutes away.

Ryken was doing great, and I was feeling good. Life felt so wonderful and normal. *Normal. What a crazy word. We are anything but normal. Whatever we are, I like it. I'll keep it.*

We took some great pictures with Ryken and Kaden. My favorite picture was Ryken sleeping on his grandpa's shoulder. My baby was so cute! Kaden was acting goofy in the pictures like a typical two year old. He made funny faces and closed his eyes. What a guy! Kaden was having so much fun, and it was such a good day. It felt good but strange to laugh again.

We headed home that evening and I said a silent prayer for my children and Brett. *Thank you, God, for my life.* On the drive home, the boys slept and Brett and I had a nice visit. The following day was Sunday, and my step-grandparents stopped in for a short visit to meet Ryken. I was not getting sick of showing him off. Kaden was always ready to ham it up and have some fun. *I sure love my boys. I am so lucky! It sure is nice to be at home instead of in the hospital. What a wonderful weekend.*

Brett went to work on Monday morning, and I was home with the boys. It was going so smoothly. We were having fun, and I was glad to be home and with Kaden again.

My only concern was that Ryken's bum seemed to be getting red. I was using some cream, but it did not seem to be helping much. He was having diarrhea off and on as well. I made sure the medicines were given as directed to decrease the side effects of the sodium benzoate. I hoped his bum would heal. I felt anxiety starting to creep in again.

CHAPTER 14

Pediatric Follow-Up Appointment

On Wednesday, November 16, we had an appointment with our pediatrician. Ryken had not been eating much since his feeding at four thirty that morning. He would nurse for a few moments before losing interest. He was quite sleepy that afternoon.

All morning, I had tried to get him to nurse. We decided to go into the city early and had lunch by the doctor's office. The drive into the city was good, and the highway conditions were great even though there was snow. Ryken slept again, and Kaden chatted with us as he played with his Hot Wheels.

At lunch, Kaden was great. I tried to nurse Ryken again, but he was still not interested. He was very sleepy, and he was developing a bad diaper rash. It was a side effect of the sodium benzoate. The rationale for the medication was that it helped bring down the glycine levels in the body. The phenobarbital was supposed to stop Ryken from having seizures. I was so thankful we would be seeing our pediatrician within the hour.

Brett and I headed up in the elevator with the boys. Ryken was dozing in his car seat. In the waiting room at the doctor's office, Kaden entertained himself with toys.

He is such an awesome kid. I watched Kaden playing and having fun.

Ryken was given a thorough checkup, and I discussed my concerns about his rash from the sodium benzoate. The doctor prescribed a special barrier cream for Ryken. It would stay on the skin and inhibit the diarrhea from doing more damage to Ryken's bum. Dr. Shomas agreed to lower the sodium benzoate dosage to see if it would decrease the diarrhea, which would help the rash.

The doctor was concerned that Ryken's muscle tone was low and that he was so lethargic. Ryken's lack of interest in breast-feeding was concerning and could lead to dehydration. He wanted to admit Ryken to the pediatrics ward overnight for closer monitoring. He called over to the hospital, and arrangements were made.

We drove to the hospital, and Ryken was admitted. We tried to get settled in our new room that afternoon. Ryken was placed in a crib that appeared too big for my tiny baby. He had been sleeping in a bassinet at home for the past nine days. Seeing him in a big crib reminded me how young he was. He was two days away from being a month old, and we were back in the hospital again. It was beginning to feel like my second home.

The nurse administered an IV, and Ryken was given fluids to avoid dehydration. We were at the back of the pediatric ward, and Ryken would be observed overnight. At least he would be monitored.

I had to admit that I was relieved. Ryken would not eat, which was beginning to concern me. On a positive note, I was glad to be around professionals who knew what they were doing. I tried to breast-feed Ryken every hour or two, but he showed little interest. Ryken's glycine levels had been dropping since the introduction of the sodium benzoate.

I was concerned that the medicine was wreaking havoc on Ryken's poor little bum. However, the medicine was supposed to bring down his glycine levels to prevent any seizures. I was torn and did not know what to do. A part of me was glad that the dosage had been lowered so his bum could heal.

We settled in, and I put my baby in the crib. I slept in a chair that folded out into a makeshift bed. It was not the most comfortable space, but I was grateful to be there with Ryken. I told myself it was better than nothing. I slept on my left side so I could face Ryken all night.

Brett and Kaden went home together for the night. It was nice to see Kaden with his daddy. The hospital was very accommodating and lent me a pump for my breast milk. There was a place on the ward to store it too. After pumping again I said good night to Brett and my boys in my mind, I sent hugs and kisses to each of them, and drifted off to sleep. I welcomed the reprieve from my complicated life.

Ryken and I slept pretty well. He was still not nursing though. I talked to our doctor about reducing Ryken's sodium benzoate since I felt it was causing the diarrhea and the awful diaper rash. I felt like it was a catch-22 because the medicine was prescribed to help lower Ryken's glycine levels, but his diaper rash was so raw that my baby was suffering. I felt like he was not interested in eating because he was in such pain. Ryken had not been crying though. It was hard to tell what was happening to my baby since he couldn't talk.

Our pediatrician agreed to lower it from 230 milligrams to 175 milligrams. With the reduction of the medicine, air on his bum (I had left his diaper off), and a good barrier cream, we began to see some improvement. Ryken was getting lots of sleep and an IV to ensure he remained hydrated. I hoped his bum would start to heal quickly.

On the second afternoon, Ryken began to show more interest in eating. I was able to nurse him a bit. He was eating better at night as well. On Thursday night, we snuggled together, and I watched "Everybody Loves Raymond" while he nursed. It was a good distraction as I rocked and snuggled Ryken to my chest.

At times, Ryken's eyes were unfocused or looked off to the side. I tried not to let it bother me. I shoved the worry and stress down into the pit of anxiety in my body that had begun shortly after his birth. The emotions knew the path to travel down and how to remain undercover. I was unable to deal with them. I tried to stay on autopilot.

The following day, Dr. Shomas told us that Ryken's lethargy might be due to an upper respiratory infection. Kaden and I had been getting over a viral infection, and we may have passed it on to Ryken. After being examined, Ryken had no fever—and his respiratory rate was normal.

On Friday, Ryken was doing much better. Tia came over at lunch to meet Ryken. I was thrilled to show him off to my friend. She was the first person from work that was able to meet him. Ryken was doing much better, and he was more alert. She held him, and my world started to feel right again.

Another cousin called and wanted to come and visit. She had not seen Ryken yet, but I asked her not to come because her son was sick. I did not want Ryken catching any other viruses, especially since he had just begun to nurse again. I needed Ryken to get strong again so we could return home.

Aunty Deann and Aunty Mindy showed up that afternoon and were able to hold and snuggle Ryken. I took a few pictures of them together.

On Saturday morning, a different pediatrician entered our room. *They must take turns working on the weekends.* I wanted another opinion on the sodium benzoate. I still had questions about how it was causing the severe diarrhea that was burning Ryken's skin. I shared my concerns about the medicine.

The pediatrician looked at me and chuckled. "Well, one of its other uses is taking tar off of tires."

I stared at him in astonishment. *Is he kidding?* I said, "Are you joking?"

"No. It was used to clean tar off of the tires on cars," he replied.

My thoughts were not good. I did not need to hear that. I was supposed to give my baby medicine that takes tar off of tires? What was that going to do to Ryken's stomach, intestinal tract, brain, and esophagus? No wonder his bum was raw.

I didn't even let Kaden have pop for crying out loud! My stomach hurt, and my anxiety started to grow. It was like a snake was twisting up my body and was going to start strangling me at any moment. It felt like a noose around my throat. I felt as though I would start hyperventilating at any moment. I told myself to calm down and breathe. I felt the snake slowly slithering away. The anxiety attack was at bay for the moment, and so was my anger.

The doctor checked Ryken and left the room. I was seething inside. I tried to remain calm. *I can't worry about my emotions. I have a job to do. I need to nurse and care for Ryken and give him this nasty medicine.* I felt sick to my stomach about giving him the sodium benzoate. In my mind's eye, I saw a tire full of tar. *And I feed this to my precious baby?*

I said a prayer and tried to prepare myself mentally. I made sure he was given the ranitidine first to help him from developing acid reflux from the sodium benzoate.

I was supposed to give it to Ryken to help him live longer, but what was I doing to him and his body while he was alive and living? Was that any way to live in the meantime: unable to eat, in pain from the severe diaper rash, and hooked up to an IV in the hospital? I was sick inside. I had to give my son's life to the doctors to manage, but I had so many concerns and issues.

That afternoon, there was a knock on the door. I was just about to go for a bath, and Brett and Ryken were going to have some time together. The door opened, and it was Kaden. I was so excited to see my beautiful son.

I hugged my big boy, and he said, "Pop."

I looked at Brett and thought I hadn't heard him correctly. "What did you say, buddy?"

Kaden said, "I had pop."

I looked at my in-laws and was so upset. Tears filled my eyes, and my throat hurt. Thoughts began to race through my mind. Kaden had never had pop. He was not allowed pop, and everyone knew it. He was only two. He barely got juice. I turned to Brett and said, "I need to go have my bath."

I left before I said anything hurtful. I burst out crying in the bathroom and tried to relax in the tub. I did some deep breathing and told myself that Kaden would be okay. *It was only pop.*

My world was starting to spin out of control again, and I did not have the remote control to stop it or slow it down. The hot water rejuvenated me and helped me decompress. For a few moments, I closed my eyes, relaxed, and lost myself in the warmth and silence of the water. It was a short escape from reality.

I was calmer when I returned to the room. We took Kaden to the playroom on the ward, and Brett's parents stayed with Ryken. Kaden drove the toy car, and we did a puzzle together. He was in good spirits.

Brett had chatted with his parents about giving Kaden pop. In their defense, they did not want Kaden feeling left out since everyone else was having pop. Brett suggested substituting juice next time. Juice would be a big treat for Kaden. I was glad he had spoken with them. I adored my in-laws—and they took very good care of Kaden—but I was struggling to make sense of my world again.

Lack of sleep and worrying constantly about Ryken had left me frail and emotional. I felt guilty about not being present for Kaden. Guilt was eating away at my core. No amount of bathing could wash it away.

We played until it was time for Kaden to leave. The hospital could be quite boring after an hour or two. I hugged him close and told him I loved him. I would see him the next day for a visit. My parents helped care for him as well. I left it to the grandparents to sort out who would care for Kaden. I was unable to organize all of them, and I trust each of them with Kaden. I thanked my in-laws for bringing him in for a visit and hugged them good-bye.

Brett went home to sleep, and Ryken and I snuggled during his late feedings. As he nursed, I watched "Everybody loves Raymond" again. I was beyond joyful that he was eating again and that he was not on intravenous anymore. His bum appeared to be healing too, which was good. I looked down at my Champion who had been through so much. I prayed that he was on the mend again.

It was nice that our family came to visit us and to watch them with Ryken. He had begun eating again and was getting back to his normal feeding schedule of every two or three hours during the day. He was still getting lots of air on his bum without a diaper and was healing fast.

On Sunday morning, we were told that we would be discharged later that day. Yeah! We were finally getting discharged after four nights and five days in pediatrics. It was long enough, and I could not wait to go back home to be with my boys again. I missed Kaden like crazy and wanted to have our life back.

We had tasted freedom for ten days after Ryken was discharged home from NICU. I could not wait to go back to living the dream of being at home with my two boys. I had thought about it throughout my pregnancy. Now that Ryken was doing well and nursing consistently, I wanted to be discharged. The skin on his bum was healed, and the barrier cream was helping. The diarrhea had subsided with the reduction in the sodium benzoate.

It was time to break free and fly the coop again. It felt like déjà vu. We were homeward bound. Hurdle number two was over. We packed up on Sunday, November 20.

While the sun set on another day, life was good again. I could take a deep breath and relax for a moment. I felt all my worries disappear. I focused on the positive and was grateful that Ryken was doing well again.

CHAPTER 15

Life at Home: Pure Bliss

M y mom came up to help for a couple days. It was helpful to have her, and I appreciated having her around. We had a great visit, and Kaden got a lot of attention. Ryken did too. We rarely put him down unless it was naptime. We were making up for all the time we never got to hold him.

The week at home flew by. Brett went to work, and I was not short on things to do. With the scheduled medicine intervals and feedings, breakfast, snack, lunch, nap, snack, and preparing meals, the days were gone in a haze.

Life was so great, and I was feeling so blessed with my boys. We all napped at the same time; thankfully, that part of our routine had not been interrupted. I loved naps and was not one to miss them. I felt so much better after resting. I was being mindful of postpartum depression. It had not found me yet. Maybe it realized I had suffered enough while watching Ryken in NICU and gave me a pass. Whatever it was, I would take it.

I was in my glory at home with Kaden and Ryken. Even though there was a bit of stress with the medications for Ryken, I took it all in stride. I wrote everything down in a special book—with the date and time and medication—and it was not confusing for me. I was still writing down Ryken's feedings and output like I did at the hospital. Everything was right on the counter. Ryken took his medications from the bottle as I rocked him in the green rocker recliner.

I was smiling. I was in pure bliss about being home with my boys and having a normal day. My normal days were what many people took completely for granted. Not me. I knew it was a gift. I loved it, and I loved my life.

As I nursed Ryken, I could hear Brett reading to Kaden. Kaden was giggling and laughing. I also heard my husband laughing. It sounded more like a party in his room than a quiet Zen moment to entice Kaden into slumber land. It was music to my ears.

I look down and say, "I love you, Ryken." I was in peace; my miracle had come true. I was home with all my boys. I thanked God for helping me. I had done enough begging that he must have thought it was "enough already." *Who said begging and praying don't work?*

Ryken took a breather from eating, and I lifted him to my chest. I kissed his cheek, snuggled him, and patted his back. I felt still inside. It was called serenity. I had been praying for those moments in the hospital. *I live in the present now. There is magic in the air, and I am complete. Life is good again.*

I basked in it and treasured the moment. I heard a loud burp in my ear. I smiled and kissed his head. "That must feel better," I said.

Ryken had released the trapped gas in his tummy and was anxious to nurse again. I switched sides and settled in to enjoy our bonding time. I stroked his hair as he ate. He was five weeks old and looked so different already. He was turning into a little pork chop. He loved to eat and was gaining weight steadily. It was nice not to worry about that anymore. People can take so much for granted when they have healthy babies.

Off to bed the boys went, and Brett and I had a few rare moments of time alone. I was so glad that I was sharing my life with him. There was something powerful between us. The difficult days in the hospital had united us like nothing else could have. *I guess the bad times can unite people just like the happy times do.* I hugged him and told him he was the best dad. I told him that our boys were so lucky to have such an amazing father. I also gave myself credit for choosing a wonderful husband. I was a smart woman. We went to bed with a glow in our eyes and love in our hearts. Life was good today.

The sun always rises. Today is no exception. It is going to be an exciting day. It's Friday, November 25. I am coping wonderfully and feeling great.

I had gotten into a routine with Ryken's medicines and feedings. He was nursing well, and his diaper rash had cleared up.

Kaden was constantly looking at Ryken and saying, "Love him. Love baby Ryken." Having my boys together was exactly how I had pictured it in my mind.

I smiled at my good fortune. I gave Kaden a hug while he played with his cars and trucks in the living room. I looked at my precious boys, and I was in awe of them. Their sweet faces and soft skin made me want to cuddle and kiss them all day long. Seeing them at home together made everything we had been through worth it.

Kaden had his baby brother, and Ryken had the best big brother in the world. All my dreams from pregnancy were coming true. They were as close as they could be. Ryken looked up adoringly to Kaden, and Kaden gushed over Ryken. When they looked into each other's eyes, they had a deep soul connection.

I decided to video my boys for the first time. It was so cute. *Why haven't I done this sooner?* Kaden was chatting like crazy. He was kissing Ryken who was staring at him.

I said, "I love you, buddy."

Kaden said, "Love you."

I said, "Who else do you love?"

He thought for a moment and looked into the camera. "Uh, self."

I laughed out loud. "Yes, buddy-boy. You should love yourself."

I must be doing something right. What is a better answer to that question from a kid whose mom is a social worker?

Ryken battled the hiccups and watched Kaden talk to me. "Else?" said Kaden. I understood my toddler as only a mother does. "Who else do you love Kaden?"

"Baby Ryken!" he replied happily in his singsong voice that also had a hint of a Boston accent. I was so full of joy that my boys had each other.

"I adore you, Kaden," I said. I gazed at Ryken with unconditional love in my eyes. *Life is good.*

I was excited for the Santa Claus parade. Brett and I were taking the boys out for supper before the parade. I couldn't wait to watch Kaden's face when he saw all the floats. I couldn't wait to see his face when he saw Santa Claus.

We all had long naps in the afternoon. It was a big deal for us to go out for supper and the parade with Ryken. *Three weeks ago, we did not think Ryken would ever come home. Thank you, God, for answering my prayers.*

Brett came home from work at five o'clock. It was perfect timing. I had just finished nursing Ryken and giving him his medications. We drove to the restaurant, and I felt like a kid in a candy store. My life was turning into the dream I had envisioned. Ryken was awake, and Brett was holding him while we decided what to order. A nice waitress took our food requests.

In no time, our food arrived. We were having a great time. You would not know a toddler and a newborn were with us. The restaurant was relatively quiet.

There was a friendly elderly couple beside our table. The woman said how beautiful Ryken was. Of course, I agreed with her. She made small talk with Kaden and commented on how cute he was as well. *This is a smart lady,* I thought.

She said, "I can hold your baby for you while you eat."

Brett said, "No that's okay. I have him." Brett held Ryken and fed himself quite easily. It was a rare moment for Brett. In Ryken's entire life, there had only been a few moments to hold Ryken and enjoy him like that.

The woman said, "Why don't you let me hold your baby so you can eat? I sure wouldn't mind."

Brett said, "Thanks, but I've got him."

Wow! This lady is persistent. I'll give her that.

Brett and I shifted in our chairs to set a physical boundary with her since words didn't appear to be working. We avoided any further eye contact with their table. We sure were getting good at setting boundaries.

She finally left us alone to enjoy our meal in peace. I felt an urge to tell her to not be offended after the hell we had been through, but I kept those words to myself. We finished our meal and headed downtown.

I said, "Why didn't you let that lady hold Ryken while you ate?"

He replied, "I was not going to let some strange lady hold Ryken. What if she dropped him on his head?" I had never thought of that.

In that moment, I saw how Ryken's experience had affected my husband. I was so proud to have him as the father of our children. I was so glad that Brett was holding Ryken when the lady asked to hold him. If I had been holding Ryken, I might have said yes to her. *What if she had accidently hurt him?*

Ryken was precious cargo. We could not let just anyone handle him. In the hospital, we had no choice what happened to him since the doctors, nurses, and medical staff were fighting for his life. Picking and prodding at him. Testing and hypothesizing his life. They were only doing their jobs, but that was our reality. There was no choice for us. Today, Brett had a choice about what would happen with Ryken.

Our little man fell asleep in his car seat and slept through the entire parade. Brett and I were able to focus on Kaden and talked about the different floats with him. The Santa float was the best. Kaden waved to Santa and smiled. His beautiful smile warmed my heart. I was feeling so blessed. His joy and excitement were contagious.

Kaden had been through a lot too. I said a silent prayer to God that Kaden would come through the experience okay. I missed Kaden so much while I was at the hospital. *That is all over now. We are all together.*

The next day was Saturday, and Kali and Erin came over with a gift for Ryken. It was so wonderful to introduce him to some of my closest friends. They stayed for an hour, and Erin snuggled with Ryken. Kaden entertained us with his chatter. The four of us enjoyed a quiet evening together.

On Sunday, my step-grandparents visited. I was grateful that they had taken the time to come over and meet our new baby.

I tucked my boys in, kissed them good night, and fell into a peaceful sleep until Ryken woke up for his nighttime feeding. I nursed and rocked my baby in our green rocker recliner while Brett and Kaden slept.

It was cold outside, but it was warm in my heart. I was feeling a breeze by the back of my head (the front door had a nasty draft). Whenever there was a north wind, it was worse. I turned on the electric fireplace and put blankets around us.

I should move the rocking chair farther away from the door. Right now, it's about four feet away. Maybe I should reconfigure the living room. I could do that this week with Mom.

I was looking forward to my mom's visit. It was amazing how life can be stressful at one moment and then switch to normal and enjoyable. After Ryken finished eating and burped, I changed his diaper. I swaddled him, kissed his cheeks, and gave him Eskimo kisses on his nose. I put him in his bassinet, and he was asleep within seconds.

"I love you, Ryken," I whispered. I slipped into bed, careful not to wake Brett. It was three o'clock, and he would be up in four hours for work. I fell asleep easily.

When the alarm went off on Monday morning, we said good-bye to Brett. The boys ate breakfast: Cheerios and milk for Kaden and medicine and breast milk for Ryken.

On November 28, my mom and I had lunch together. That afternoon, Brett picked us up to see the pediatrician. I was so thankful that his work was so accommodating about the doctor appointments. My mom stayed home with Kaden, and we went for a check-up with our pediatrician.

Dr. Shomas told us that Ryken's glycine levels had increased a bit since the sodium benzoate medication had been lowered. The levels were still in the normal range though. I was happy to hear the news. I was also happy the medicine would not be increased.

I notified the doctor that Ryken had been doing well at home and eating without any issues. I shared that I was very happy that the sodium benzoate was reduced. Ryken's bowel movements have improved, and there was no more diarrhea or diaper rash.

Dr. Shomas noticed that Ryken was more alert and active. Ryken had gained weight, and his cranium was normal with a soft anterior fontanel. I hung on to those words with glee. During the appointment, Ryken had an occasional "mild startle." He did fix briefly with his eyes, but he did not follow with his eyes. Dr. Shomas commented that Ryken's muscle tone was good. One concern the doctor had was that Ryken had a significant head lag.

We will just have to build up your neck muscles, little buddy. There's some tummy time at home for you, mister. I wonder how you will like that, my little man. We snuggled him so much, and I had never put him on the floor for tummy time. *No wonder your poor muscles are not working as well as they could, Ryken. That is an easy fix.*

The doctor left us with instructions to have more blood work done on Ryken in two days to check his glycine levels.

On December 1, I would take Ryken into the hospital lab to have his blood drawn to check his glycine and phenobarbital levels. We would see Dr. Shomas again in a few weeks for another follow-up appointment.

My mom and I were doing dishes that evening, and I said, "Do you think there was any damage to Ryken's brain? He appears fine to me." I was holding Ryken, swaying from side to side, and caressing his little fingers.

My mom smiled, leaned down, and kissed Ryken's little head. She said, "We would love him the same no matter what."

I felt a bit of relief from her answer, but I have a knot in my stomach. I looked down at my baby and kissed him. I gave him Eskimo kisses and kissed his cheeks and lips. "I love you, Ryken." He was perfect to me.

I handed Ryken off to Brett, and they rocked and snuggled on the green recliner. I thought about asking Brett to do tummy time with Ryken, but I thought time together was just as important. Kaden was happily playing with his toy cars on the floor beside them. He had always had a great imagination. I felt blessed and happy to be alive as I looked upon the men in my life.

I finished cleaning up and thought about how right my mom was. If Ryken were a bit delayed due to some kind of brain damage, it would not matter. *He is here—alive—and I cannot imagine life without him. Our miracle happened.* I focused on that.

A smile formed at the corners of my mouth. I felt very peaceful and calm.

CHAPTER 16

What Is Happening?

My mom had slept over, and Brett was off to work for the day. My mom and I hung out at home, playing with Kaden and snuggling Ryken. We decided to do some shopping. I completed the routine of medicine and nursing for Ryken while she prepared a snack for Kaden. We went shopping, and Ryken slept the entire time. We headed home and had lunch together.

I gave Ryken his medicine and nursed him. After he finished eating, I noticed that Ryken seemed to be gasping a bit for air. It looked hard to breathe for him.

I immediately called Brett at work, and he was home in ten minutes. In the meantime, I called Brita to see if she was available to give Ryken a treatment. I grabbed our diaper bag and kissed Kaden good-bye. "Thank you, Mom, for being here!"

Brett drove to Brita's home, and I held Ryken in the backseat. I knew it was against the law, but I couldn't bear to put him in his car seat. He seemed uncomfortable and was crying. I prayed to God that Ryken would be okay.

Brita began with his feet and touched them gently. She told us it was his lungs, and she couldn't help with that.

As we drove to the hospital, I rocked Ryken back and forth. I was unable to release him and wanted to give Ryken some comfort. I wanted him to feel my arms around him and know he was not alone.

Brett pulled up to the emergency doors, and I rushed inside with Ryken. We were taken in right away, and I handed my baby over to the medical staff. It began again. He was placed on a big hospital bed and was surrounded by doctors and nurses. He was out of my hands and out of my reach. I watched in a helpless state of confusion and dread with tears streaming down my face. He was being bagged again because of his breathing, and I overheard the doctor saying he was "acidosis." *Now what? What does that mean?*

Brett and I held each other. Motionless again. Trapped in time.

I heard "need to stabilize him" and "need bicarb." I didn't know what was happening. We were asked questions, and we tried to answer them to the best of our ability. We notified them that he had been diagnosed with nonketotic hyperglycinemia. He was doing well after his last feeding, but shortly after lunch, Ryken had difficulty with his breathing.

Ryken was moved upstairs to the intensive care unit. He was in critical condition. Brett and I said nothing. We looked at each other, but no words were exchanged. I didn't even know what to say.

I collected the diaper bag, and we followed Ryken's gurney to the intensive care unit. We were just down the hall from NICU.

As evening approached, we still had no answers. Ryken was not eating, and they hooked him up to an IV. I had been down to NICU to pump in the rooms and store the milk in the fridge. I walked down the wide hallway, picked up the phone, and called so the door could be unlocked. I entered the quietness of the intensive care unit. That was where patients of all ages went when they were very sick.

Brett was keeping a vigil at Ryken's bedside. Ryken was the only baby in there.

It was getting late, and I asked the nurse if there were cots that could be brought into Ryken's room.

She looked at me and said, "You can't stay in here. It's against policy."

I didn't think I heard her right. I asked, "You mean I can't stay the night with Ryken?"

"No. You can stay until midnight, and then you can come back at six."

I felt sick to my stomach. I began to panic; we had never been apart. I felt a knot of anxiety, and I was having trouble breathing. I already didn't understand what was going on with my baby, and now I had to leave his side due to "policy." I felt as though I was going to throw up. I began to cry.

I regained my composure and forced myself to walk outside of the unit. I called Jenna who lived on the east side of the city. It was a twenty minute drive without traffic to her home. I told her not to wait up. We wouldn't leave the hospital until midnight and would just go directly to their spare bedroom to sleep. I wanted to be back at the hospital by six and would not see her in the morning either.

She asked, "What is going on with Ryken?"

I said, "I don't know. We have not been told anything." She understood my pain, and I got to be my moody, grouchy self because I was feeling lost. *A best friend loves you no matter your mood—and they are there for you no matter what is happening in your life.*

Ryken was in a crib that was too big for his tiny body; there was a familiar sense of pain in the air. Ryken was heavily sedated the whole time. At midnight, we left the hospital. Leaving Ryken almost killed me. I cried during the whole drive.

At Jenna's house, Brett fell asleep right away. I stayed awake, thought of Ryken, and wept. I wept at the audacity of being separated from him. I wept at being separated from Kaden again. I wept for my pain of the unknown. I cried for him, for myself, for Brett, and for Kaden. I did not sleep even though I tried. I told myself that I needed to—for Ryken and myself. Sleep simply evaded me, while insomnia set in.

The alarm went off at five thirty, and I had not slept a wink. Somehow, I felt fine. Adrenaline was racing through me on the drive back to the hospital. As I walked the halls toward Ryken, I could feel the anxiety rising like a phoenix from the ashes. I couldn't wait to see him and be near him. I blew the ashes down to intermingle with all the other awful emotions I had sent that way. I would deal with them at a later time.

As we entered Ryken's room, the nurses were shaving his head. I felt anger that they were doing that to him. They told us that they needed to shave his head so they could use the veins for his IV. They put some of his hair in a plastic bottle with an orange lid for me. It was the same type of bottle I had used for my urine sample when I was pregnant. That felt like eons ago.

I felt the anger seeping into my veins. I willed it away. I pushed it down into the unknown. The silver lining was that I had a keepsake to remind me of this hospital stay. *I guess I will be able to share this with Ryken when he is older and we talk about his first haircut.*

I know the nurses were just doing their jobs, but it was still annoying. I was sure having an IV in his head was not going to be comfortable, but I told myself that they were doing what was best for my baby.

I stroked his cheeks and touched his hair. They had shaved the side of his head into a weird Mohawk. He was so bloody cute that it did not matter what his hair looked like. I was annoyed that they never asked us if they could do it. It was back to being a bystander in Ryken's life as the medical team made all the decisions and determined all the shots. The logical part of my brain knew why but I couldn't get the emotional side to understand. The tears just came, and it did not help that I had not slept in twenty-four hours. I needed sleep to cope with any form of stress.

Today was the worst form of stress, and I gave myself a break. Eventually the well of tears went dry.

Ryken was heavily sedated and sleeping quietly. I stroked his hand when they were done. I went down the hall to pump again. Brett and I hunkered down for the day; we had no idea what to expect.

I was so tired, and cried all day. When the tears left, a new set of tears showed up. Our life was a quiet waiting game. Ryken was still in critical condition, and we didn't know why.

Brett and I went to the cafeteria for a quick lunch. Brett returned to the ICU while I pumped again. The pediatrician came in to talk to us. It was the same doctor who told me about the sodium benzoate taking tar off of car tires. I was still angry with him, but I told myself to put the "tar comment" aside for now. He had no news, and there was no change in Ryken, but it was no time to hold a grudge.

He did share with us that they had decided to discontinue the sodium benzoate. They were questioning whether the sodium benzoate was causing Ryken's acidosis. My anger began to rise, but as luck would have it, my happiness quelled it. Since I was not a doctor, I had to allow myself to trust the professionals and follow their recommendations.

Now Ryken can begin healing. My concern now was what will happen to Ryken if his glycine levels get too high? There was no reply. Only silence.

CHAPTER 17

An Unexpected Meeting: Divine Intervention

B rett and I decided to eat supper in the cafeteria. I was diligent about keeping up my milk supply for Ryken. I stored my breast milk in NICU for when Ryken was ready to nurse again. We ate quickly and hurried back to the second floor to be with our baby.

As we stepped off the elevator, it was eerily quiet. There was not another person around. We walked the short distance to the secure doors of the intensive care unit. As we were approaching, they swung open.

One of our neonatal nurses who had worked with Ryken recognized us. The concern on her face was evident. She said, "Is Ryken in here now?"

Brett and I said, "Yes." I felt the tears coming again.

She looked us in the eye and asked, "What is going on with him?"

I said, "We don't know. I don't think the doctors know either."

She said, "You don't have to stay here."

I said, "What?"

Her next words would forever change the direction of our lives. "You can ask to be sent to a children's hospital to find out what is going on with Ryken."

We have a choice? Ryken has a choice? We were able to advocate for our baby by requesting that he be assessed at a children's hospital.

"They might know what is happening with him."

"Really?" My eyes pooled with tears and grew as big as saucers. It felt like she had given us a key to a locked door. Hearing that we had a right to request to go somewhere else for care for our baby was unbelievable. No one had ever told us that important piece of information. We almost missed out on connecting with her. I knew it was divine intervention. That chance meeting was anything but chance. The universe had placed her right within our path to help us help Ryken. *Thank you, God.*

We would find some answers for Ryken. We thanked her, and she wished us luck.

I wanted to hug her as hard as I could, but we all had business to do. We strode into the locked doors of the intensive care unit with confidence because we had just been given some guidance about how to help Ryken. We felt empowered and knew exactly what we needed to do for him.

Brett and I walked directly into Ryken's room. We looked down at our son in the big crib. We felt the weight of the world on our shoulders. We were trying to do the best for him, but now we knew we could help him. We needed to advocate for him. Brett and I spoke quietly as we stood by our baby's bed. It did not take us long to decide what to do. A nurse entered Ryken's room, and we told her we wanted to speak with the doctor immediately.

Within minutes, we were meeting with the pediatrician who had Ryken's CAT scans.

I looked him in the eye and said, "What do these CAT scans mean? What is going on with Ryken?"

He said, "I don't know."

I knew he was being truthful. He might not have all the answers. I gained a lot of respect for him in those moments. He was not God, and he wasn't trying to act like he was either. It must be difficult to be a doctor in moments like that.

Brett said, "We want to go to a place that would know. We want to be transferred to a children's hospital."

The doctor replied, "Okay."

Just like that. There was no begging or arguing.

The doctor went to the phone at the main desk to make arrangements. I did not know where we would be going, but I knew we would be leaving. Knowing we had other options was encouraging. I was riding the waves of hope again. By asking to go to a children's hospital, I felt we were doing the best we could for Ryken. He would be on the mend again soon, and he could go home again.

Brett and I continued our bedside vigil. I did not know which cities even had children's hospitals. I asked God for help again. I prayed that we would have a strong and knowledgeable medical team for Ryken wherever we went. I had to trust in God and that he would help us get to the best place for our precious baby.

I was feeling stronger. I knew we would be going soon. I had a belief in God, but it was beginning to fade. I had been feeling alone and abandoned by him. My faith in him was growing a bit stronger at this turn of events. I still had many questions for him. I wanted to know what Ryken had done to deserve this. And what had Brett and I done?

I went back to gratitude for the nurse. No one had ever shared that type of knowledge with us. Ryken's life was going to be different because of her. Thank you, earth angel!

Her beautiful face was permanently etched in my mind. She will always be one of my earth angels. She was sent to us in our desperate time of need. I know God and our angels sent her to us. When hope and faith were failing and we had nowhere to turn, she was like a lighthouse for us.

Maybe God had not abandoned us after all. Maybe he wanted to help Ryken. I was so tired and full of fear that I didn't even know what to believe. I was just trying to maintain my composure, keep it all together, and remain strong for Ryken.

Within minutes, we were meeting with the doctor again. He told us that a children's hospital had accepted Ryken. Ryken and I would be flying out by air ambulance in the next few hours.

We thanked him for his help. I held no more animosity toward him. I felt extremely grateful for how fast he had helped us to get Ryken the help he needed.

We immediately went back to Ryken's bedside. We contacted our parents to let them know the plan. We had to make sure there was a stable plan of care for Kaden for the next few days. We had no idea what to expect when we got to the children's hospital—or how long the stay would be. Brett's dad planned to drive through the night with him. They would meet us at the hospital in the morning.

Brett held Ryken while the nurse completed the paperwork for the transfer. I watched him hold Ryken in his arms, and tears of anguish filled my eyes. *Where does this road lead next?*

After all the signatures were completed, Brett went home and packed. I had written out a list of what I would need: underwear, socks, pajamas, sweatshirt, T-shirts, hairbrush, deodorant, comfy pants, and whatever else he thought would be helpful.

I would see him in nine hours, and I hoped we would have some answers. We hugged good-bye. He leaned down and softly kissed Ryken's cheek. Pain and uncertainty started to creep up into my throat. I willed it down because I had to go pump again. Every moment away from Ryken caused me severe anxiety.

I returned, breasts empty, but I was carrying a heavy heart. I watched the nurses prep Ryken for the flight. I stared at my baby, and little waves of helplessness washed over me again. I could not help him right then or make anything better for him. Even though he could not hear me, I told him in my mind that he would be better soon and that he would be back home with his big brother. I sent him prayers and hoped he could feel my love. I could not touch him or talk to him, but I hoped Ryken knew he was not alone. I was three feet away, and I was praying with all I had left in me.

I felt a small sense of empowerment. I hoped our new doctor would have an answer for us and would be able to help. The roller coaster of ups and downs was turning into everyday life for us. It was our new normal.

CHAPTER 18

Off to the Children's Hospital

J ust before midnight, there were many people in the room. Many orders were being given. Ryken was given a soother and was placed in the Isolette for transfer. He was hooked up to some monitors, and his vital signs were stable.

Ryken was being moved out of the intensive care unit, and I walked beside him. I was watching everyone do their best to care and transport him. He was going to be transferred with supplemental oxygen and an IV.

The universe had answered my prayers. We were heading in the direction of certainty and help. Figuring out a plan for Ryken and having a clear picture of what the next step was my plea to God.

An ambulance took us to the airport. The roads were bumpy. I was allowed to sit across from Ryken, but I was unable to touch him. We arrived at the airport, and it was so cold outside. A plane was waiting for us, ready to go.

Getting on the plane and watching so many strangers handle Ryken's Isolette was difficult. I told myself that they were all professionals. I needed to trust them. I tried to push away the fear of him being shifted or jolted. It was unnerving. I really wanted to hold Ryken for the flight, but I couldn't.

I was afraid of flying and of the turbulence disturbing Ryken's breathing. Thank God for numbness. I carried it with me everywhere I went. I had no sense of control in my life.

At least we were finally going to get answers and assistance for Ryken. My prayer was that we would finally know what was going on. We were going to a children's hospital for expertise and answers.

This is going to be helpful for us.

I glanced out the window at the big city lights. I prayed for a safe flight and landing. I prayed that Ryken would be okay during the transfer. I was hoping that we had made the right decision for him. I kept praying. It was the only thing that was helping me remain calm. My body ached from being overtired, but I couldn't sleep.

We landed, and Ryken appeared to be doing fine. There were no beeps or buzzing noises. *So far, so good.* We were met right away at the airport by an ambulance. Ryken was transported out of the airplane, and we were hit by the minus-thirty-degree temperatures. Ryken was tucked into the new ambulance and was admitted into the neonatal intensive care unit enroute to the hospital.

Ryken's oxygen levels had begun to desaturate and were in the eighties. He was still lethargic and difficult to arouse. He was placed on 100 percent oxygen. I looked at my baby and prayed. I prayed even though I didn't know if I believed in prayers anymore. It was out of habit. Maybe on another level, I knew it helped Ryken—and helped me too. I was unsure and overwhelmed. I knew that praying kept me focused and in control of my emotions. I was back on the roller coaster, and I could not derail.

The stopping and starting stressed me out as the ambulance made its way to our destination. I stared at Ryken, praying he would get there okay. I was unable to touch him. He was in a completely sealed and enclosed bassinet. I sent him words of encouragement and told him that everything was going to be okay shortly. We would have answers soon—and he would feel better.

He would be home before he knew it and be back with his big brother. The message was for me as well, and I remained calm and in control of my emotions.

I told Ryken that he would be snuggling with us in the green rocker recliner soon. "You'll be snug as a bug in your bassinet for naptime. We are here to get you better and help you recover from whatever is going on in your body. This acidosis condition that is affecting your body now will get fixed at the new hospital. Hang in there, buddy. I love you, Ryken. I love you, Ryken. I love you, Ryken."

I sat across from him and stared at his beautiful face. I was glad he had taken a soother. I hoped it was comforting for him when he was unable to feel my touch or hear my voice.

We arrived at the hospital and parked underground. Ryken was taken out of the ambulance and wheeled through many corridors. We took an elevator to the neonatal intensive care unit. There was a long hallway with many office doors on either side. At the end of this long corridor, we finally entered the unit.

I thought we were going to a pediatric unit? The sound from Ryken's nineteen days of life in the NICU back home returned to my ears. The familiar sounds didn't bring me much comfort. I was triggered, but I kept myself in check. I knew that I was supposed to trust right now. I took a deep breath in and maintained my control.

Ryken was brought to the northeast corner of the unit. There was so much hustle and bustle around him. Ryken was in acute respiratory distress. A team was working on him trying to sort out his breathing. I felt a familiar pain in my chest. It was the pain of being a mother and feeling completely helpless as I watched this new medical team help my baby live.

Ryken's blood pressure remained stable, but his acidosis still needed to be corrected. His condition was unstable, and they were having difficulty controlling it with medications. I was notified that Ryken was in critical condition at this point.

He was pale and arched when they handled or touched him. He was still able to suck on his soother, which brought me some comfort.

It was three o'clock in the morning, and I was exhausted. I meet Ryken's night nurse, Kassandra. She was petite and capable. I watched her for fifteen minutes, and she was very efficient. I was in awe of her, and she gained my trust instantly. I said a prayer of gratitude that she was my baby's nurse. I felt so much better knowing he was in the hands of such an amazing caregiver.

I looked into her brown eyes and knew in my heart that my baby was in safe hands. I had no choice. It felt better knowing intuitively that I trusted her with my son. It was nice to feel calm in my heart and know in my mind that he was safe. I said another prayer to thank God that Kassandra was Ryken's nurse.

I'd always trusted my gut instinct. My baby was in good hands, and two days of sleep deprivation required a long nap. I was on the brink of total exhaustion. I remained on the peripheral watching and praying.

CHAPTER 19

The Family Room

Normally, Ryken would have gone to the pediatric unit of the hospital, but they were full. Ryken was situated in the back with the most critical babies. There was a frenzy of activity as he was hooked up to the machines that would help him. The nurses were very calm and efficiently catered to Ryken's every need. The sounds in the NICU triggered a flood of memories for me.

I stayed by Ryken's side until I felt comfortable leaving him in Kassandra's capable hands. It did not take long.

The head doctor of neonatal introduced himself and shook my hand. His name is Dr. Nolan Uchi and his plan at the moment was to try to correct the metabolic acidosis, which was causing Ryken's distress. He notified me that he would also be consulting with the head of metabolics, neuroradiology, and neurology for Ryken's care.

Dr. Uchi wanted to discuss Ryken's brain, but I respectfully interrupted him. I asked him if he would wait until Brett arrived. I was so tired physically and emotionally that I could not hear anything without Brett by my side.

Dr. Uchi was very kind and agreed to wait. I was thankful since my reserves were on empty. I was on the brink of insanity. I asked about a pump since I was completely engorged. I was taken to the "family room" to rest. It was a hop, skip, and a jump away from Ryken. I said a silent prayer of thanks to the heavens.

In the spacious room, there was a rocker recliner, a loveseat, and a small fridge. A small desk was in the far corner. The desk had a phone and an alarm clock. To the right of a window, there was a queen-sized bed with a white and yellow flowered comforter. It was like a gift from heaven. Dr. Uchi left the room after confirming our meeting with Brett.

I sat on the bed and relaxed. Ryken was in capable hands, and I could rest for a moment. I was right beside Ryken. If he needed me, they could come get me.

A nurse knocked on the door and brought me a pump. *God bless her soul!* I was so engorged and in such pain that pumping would be a welcomed relief. I quickly began pumping and placed the milk in the fridge. I would be able to give it to Ryken when he began eating again.

I closed my eyes and welcomed sleep, knowing my boys were in good hands. *Good night, Kaden and Ryken. I love you. Drive safe, Brett and Grandpa. See you soon.*

Sleep engulfed me and pried me away from my life. The family room was a welcome haven from the chaos I was in. A bed to lie down on and close my eyes had never felt so good.

CHAPTER 20

Finding Answers

As though only moments had flown by rather than hours, Brett woke me at 7:02 am. The four hours of sleep made a big difference for me. I got up, and we went to see Ryken. We held his little hand and kissed his soft cheek. I stroked his blond hair and whispered, "I love you." I asked him how he was doing, knowing we would get no response. I needed him to hear me and know that I was there for him.

"Rest and heal, my champion. Soon we will have answers for you." I kissed his cheek again and touched his hair, feeling the softness of it. My heart sent love and light to Ryken.

I willed my mind to stay positive but we were told that there had been no change in his condition.

With heavy hearts we went to meet with Dr. Uchi in his office. Brett's dad went to the family room to rest after the long drive. Brett had driven most of the night, but he was his usual strong and steady self. His essence gave me strength and I was relieved that he was at the hospital with me now. We stepped inside the doctor's office and sat down together, quietly side by side. Introductions were made as there was a pediatric neurologist in the room for the meeting as well.

Brett and I waited expectantly to hear how these doctors could help Ryken. They would give us a clear picture of which way to go next. My heart was bursting with hope. Feeling somewhat refreshed from my sleep, I listened with anticipation. I was on the edge of my seat and holding onto a prayer.

Dr. Uchi explained that Ryken was still in critical condition. The lactic acidosis was barely under control, and they had not found where it was originating. The medications they were using were barely keeping the lactic acidosis at bay. Ryken was definitely not getting better yet. If they stopped the infusions to try to correct the lactic acidosis, the acidosis would eventually cause multisystem failure and cardiac arrest.

Dr. Uchi paused and took a deep breath. "We have taken new MRIs of Ryken's brain since your arrival. The nonketotic hyperglycinemia has caused Ryken's seizures. These seizures have caused brain damage."

Part of me was surprised at that news, but a deeper part of me was not.

The next few moments dramatically changed our lives forever.

"The prognosis of Ryken's condition is grim," Dr. Uchi said.

My world started closing in on me.

We went to that hospital for answers. We were given a very cut-and-dry, black-and-white response. They painted a clear picture for us. We were being steered down a fork in the road that we had no choice but to travel down.

Dr. Uchi said, "Ryken's entire brain was damaged. The only part of his brain that has not been damaged yet is the brain stem. The brain stem is the part of the brain that controls the same reflexes that a baby does. These reflexes—sucking or sticking out your tongue—would be normal reflexes in a baby Ryken's age. Sadly, that is all he will ever be able to do. Ryken will never come off of life support. The next step is that eventually he will need a tracheotomy."

The movie reel in my brain was projecting pictures of my sweet baby hooked up to machines and waiting for his throat to be cut open to help with his breathing. There would never be any improvement. We could look forward to a tracheotomy, but he would never come home again.

This can't be real. These words can't be true.

When I looked into Dr. Uchi's eyes, I knew that he had chosen each word carefully. My worst nightmare had come true—and that was my new reality.

Brett and I talked calmly and quietly. Our words were the same. It was as though we had been given the same script to read. We expressed that—in no uncertain terms—we would not have Ryken live like that. Living on life support provided no quality of life for our baby. We did not want Ryken to suffer anymore or have a tracheotomy. We wanted him taken off of life support. That was no way to live, especially for a baby. Our baby. Our beautiful baby boy. Our champion, Ryken Addison.

We knew what was best for him without discussing it. Our wedding song, "When You Say Nothing At All" by Allison Krauss, took on a new meaning for our marriage in that moment. Brett and I were in sync. We thought alike, which was a godsend. If either of us had thought differently, it would have been another difficult road to travel down. If either of us did not want Ryken taken off of life support, it would have been another problem to contend with. Thank you, God. It was a small miracle, but it was not the miracle I had been praying for.

The neurologist and Dr. Uchi showed us Ryken's brain on the CAT scans. We were able to see how the seizures had affected his brain. The doctors pointed out exactly where it was damaged, and it was not a pretty picture. The entire brain showed the effects of what the seizures had done.

Looking at the X-rays was heartbreaking. It was like running a hundred miles an hour and hitting a brick wall.

It was a very clear jolt of reality. There was no arguing with a scan of a brain and seeing how each part of it was hurt.

The truth we were facing was that Ryken's entire brain was damaged—not just a few parts. The visual images shook me to the reality of the situation. The full realization hit me again. There was no fixing this. There was no miracle for me, for us, or for Ryken.

The pain was so monumental that I went into a state of shock. I had been in shock on October 28 when we were told about the nonketotic hyperglycinemia. Life had given us some hope since that day, and I had been hanging onto it for dear life. That hope was slipping through my hands quickly. I furiously tried to grasp it. I tried to stop it from falling away from me, but it was pointless. It was out of my reach. It was like sand slipping through an hourglass.

The idea that Ryken would not be there someday was unimaginable, but that was the conversation we were having.

In a few moments, my life changed forever. There was no wondering. There was no second-guessing. This beautiful baby of ours was never going home. We came here to find answers. The answer was that Ryken would have no quality of life on earth. He would never grow up and play hockey. He would never go to school, graduate, get married, have children, have a career, or become a grandparent. Nothing. Nothing! Nothing!

Part of me was slipping away as my heart began to crumble. "The heart knows no bounds" took on a new meaning for me. My love and protectiveness for Ryken grew a thousand times in those moments, yet I knew he would be gone soon. I would be unable to express it or share it with him.

We wanted answers, and within twelve hours, we knew what we were up against. It was the abyss of nothing. There would be no improvement. There was no miracle.

Moving forward would be a life in intensive care—hooked up to tubes and monitors. The only thing Ryken had to look forward to in life was the possibility of a tracheotomy.

Doesn't that sound like fun? More cutting into my baby? More poking and prodding? Are you kidding me?

The doctor explained the options for removal of the machines and intubation. It was decided that Ryken would be removed from the machines the following afternoon. We had until then to say our good-byes.

We consented to the do-not-resuscitate order. Dr. Uchi explained that in the event of cardiopulmonary arrest, there would be no compressions or bolus epinephrine to get Ryken's heart going again. He would be allowed to die without medical intervention. Ryken was in such dire straits that he might die before anyone had a chance to say good-bye to him.

There was no way he should have to suffer anymore when he would not get better. It would be selfish of us to keep him on life support so we could have him alive. He would be "alive," but he would not be "living." He would have "life," but he would not be "full of life."

CHAPTER 21

Baptized: United or Catholic? Flip a Coin

All the cards were on the table, and there was nowhere to run. The truth shall set you free. The truth had set Ryken free from a life of suffering and pain. He would be released from his pain, but our suffering was about to begin. I did not have time to think about that. There was a lot to do, and time was running out.

We went to the family room to make our calls. With a heavy heart, I called our parents, siblings, and a few close friends to let them know the worst possible news had come true. Ryken would be taken off of life support the following day, December 3. If they wanted to come say good-bye, they were welcome to. I asked if they could bring their cameras since mine was in the diaper bag at home. I had nothing with me but a pair of pajamas, a toothbrush, and a few changes of clothes. I did not think to put it on the list for Brett to bring. I wished I had only asked for the camera so I could take pictures of our last days together.

Ryken was not even seven weeks old. They told us he could possibly have six months. I thought we had more time. I thought we would have the six months like the other baby with the same condition.

The reality was that I still believed we had forever with him. I had believed he would outlive me. I did not believe the doctors or what they told me. I was still living in the land of hope whenever I could. I was living on Denial Street.

Hope had been my best friend for weeks until she betrayed me. She lit up my illusions with a gasoline-soaked match. My life was going up in flames, and my dreams were turning to ashes before my very eyes.

After the calls, we went back to sit with Ryken. They decided just before lunch that Ryken needed to be intubated again. Brett and I left the unit while they performed the procedure. I could not watch. I felt such a loss of control. I was tiptoeing beside the edge of sanity. Watching Ryken get intubated would put me over the edge and into the welcoming arms of insanity that I felt were beckoning me. Taunting me. A part of me wanted to go there, but I forbade it. I was listening to my higher self, and I was out of harm's way for now.

The next topic was whether we wanted Ryken baptized. If the answer were yes, then arrangements would have to be made that day. We were not choosing to baptize Ryken out of fear that God would not welcome Ryken into heaven because he was not baptized. He would be baptized out of a purely selfish want. We chose to baptize him for one reason only: I wanted to have a ritual performed for him that we would have done anyway under normal circumstances. We would have had Ryken baptized United just like Kaden.

Ryken would have worn Kaden's three-month-old white baptismal suit. We would have had our younger brother and sister as his godparents. Ryken would have been baptized in the United Church with close family and friends in attendance just like Kaden. It was about doing something special for Ryken.

It was arranged to have Ryken baptized later that day, right after lunch. We had requested that he be baptized United if possible. The faith Ryken would be baptized in would depend on the minister or priest who was working that day. Now we would have no choice about the religion. Rather than be mad, I focused on being grateful that Ryken could be baptized. I said a silent prayer that Ryken was still alive to do this one thing for him in a few hours.

We were notified that today it was a Catholic priest on duty. Arrangements would be made, and we were learning to go with the flow of things as they happened. That was not hard when a person is walking around in a haze of despair and sadness. We were happy that we could do something for Ryken. Our youngest brother and sister were going to be his godparents. I wrote the names on the piece of paper before the priest began speaking.

We stood around Ryken's bassinet, and I stared at Ryken as tears filled my eyes. I really wasn't hearing the words of the priest. With Grandpa, Brett, and I in attendance, Ryken was baptized in the Catholic faith within minutes.

Now it was time to prepare him to enter into the kingdom of heaven. That phrase sounds ridiculous to me now. Before my world was turned upside down, "the kingdom of heaven" was a just a phrase to me. I had seen the words, but I'd never had to internally process the meaning.

I was preparing for our baby to leave our world and enter heaven. The words were not comforting at all because I wanted Ryken's kingdom to be on earth—with us. I wanted Ryken to preside in our kingdom with King Kaden and our own royal family.

We would have to plan his funeral next. I did not know how soon it would be. I pushed that thought into the crevices of my mind. It was trapped in the dusty corner, an abandoned thought, covered up, and disposed of until the time came to dig it back up and deal with it. Only time would tell. I hated that saying. I hated it because I was running out of time with Ryken.

That evening, the hours flew by. All of the people in our immediate families that were able to came to the hospital to say good-bye to Ryken. They drove late into the night in bitterly cold weather to get to the children's hospital, which was seven hours away. That Friday would forever be Black Friday to me. Doomsday.

Our parents, siblings, and Jenna began arriving around 4 am on Saturday morning. I watched as they took turns going over to Ryken's bassinet, touching his hands, and saying good-bye. It was a very humbling experience for me.

Our nurse offered to do Ryken's hand and feet molds for us. We agreed, and I felt better knowing I would have something to hold when Ryken was gone. We continued our bedside vigil with Ryken. Our family took turns with him while we met with genetic counselors and social workers.

At 10:30 am, Ryken's lactic acidosis improved, which was good news. My heart took a leap of faith—until we were notified that Ryken was still deteriorating neurologically. He was less active and was arching and posturing more. A nerve exam was done, and Ryken had no gag reflex, no sucking, and no grasping. He failed other tests as well. When he was taken off of the ventilator, his breathing was rapid and irregular. He took spontaneous breaths. He was desaturating to 30 percent oxygen. The end of his time on life support was drawing near. I knew we had made the right decision after listening to the doctor's examination.

The leap of faith left my heart as quickly as it came, and it took all my hope with her. I was living moment by moment and trying my hardest to be present with Ryken during the time I had left with him.

The next conversation was that Ryken would be kept as comfortable as possible with no suffering. We expressed our concerns and asked that Ryken be removed from all machines, including the tubes. In order for Ryken to have no pain, we were notified that he would receive morphine intravenously.

Dr. Uchi discussed the importance of having a skin, muscle, and liver biopsies done on Ryken to help with the diagnosis of the metabolic condition. The biopsies would be sent away for testing to pinpoint the exact mutation of the gene for nonketotic hyperglycinemia. That would allow for the possibility of prenatal testing in the future, which was essential if we wanted to have more biological children.

Dr. Uchi arranged for us to have a meeting with the head doctor of metabolics. Her name was Dr. Sasha Westbrook. She was petite and kind. Her voice was calm and she exuded confidence. I felt that I could trust her, as she was very knowledgeable. Dr. Westbrook and her team explained the magnitude and importance of the biopsies. We were at a children's hospital, and all the professionals were at our fingertips to help us.

The next thing to contend with was saying no to other family and friends who wanted to visit us at the hospital. We said no for two very important reasons. First, I wanted as much time with Ryken as possible. I did not want to share him with anyone else. It was hard enough sharing him with the grandparents and siblings.

Second, I needed space from the world, and I did not want to visit with anyone. Time was ticking, and we were running out of it. Not knowing how long we had with him made our time with him even more precious.

For the rest of December 3, Ryken remained on life support. The doctors, genetic counselors, and social workers tried to piece together the puzzle of NKH for us. They were explaining what they could about this condition as well as what that meant for us moving forward as carriers. In each future pregnancy, there would be a 25 percent chance that our baby would have NKH.

The counselors asked if there was any way that Brett and I could be related. If by chance—somewhere down the line—we were distant cousins or distant relatives. There was no way we were. I knew it in my soul, but Brett and I were each carrying this rare genetic condition. It was bizarre and disheartening all at the same time.

In addition to losing Ryken, there might be no more babies for us. There was no guarantee they would find anything in Ryken's DNA that would help in prenatal testing. It was a shot in the dark, and they were looking for a needle in a haystack. They needed to find the exact code in Ryken's DNA so that they would know what to look for in the DNA of any future babies. They were betting on the biopsies for answers. The neonatal classic form condition would always have the outcome of a death sentence for our babies.

The next baby could be worse than Ryken. The next baby could suffer more than Ryken had suffered, which would be hard to fathom. *How is this all possible?* The reality of what I was hearing sunk into my brain.

Like pushing pennies into pudding, the pennies disappear. The words were falling into the abyss of my brain, but I was on sensory overload. A lot of the information was getting lost. The words used to describe everything did not make sense to me.

The news was like a blow to the head or a shot between the eyes. The counselors were very kind and knowledgeable. They spoke with a lot of compassion, which was very thoughtful.

I felt as though they were wearing their kid gloves to explain everything to us. They treated us with empathy while their words hit us in our hearts. Our parents and siblings sat in on some of the meetings. It was easier than trying to explain it to them later on since we could barely understand it ourselves.

I thought about how I would dislike their role if I were in their positions. It would be a real crummy job. It would be great when you can help a family or see a baby get better. It would be hard when there was nothing you could do to help them. I will always be grateful for their compassion.

I was trying to process everything. In the back of my mind, I was absorbing the fact that Ryken would die soon. I did not want to hear any more bad news, but I was unable to say it to anyone. Obviously they needed to tell us the information, but I just wanted to go back and be with my baby before he died. I did not share those words out loud.

I hated the idea of operating on Ryken and cutting into him. It made me sick, and I was so anxious that I wanted to throw up. I had to tell my brain to stop thinking about it. I did not want to lose control of my emotions.

It was a difficult decision for us. We were so overwhelmed, but we understood that they were trying to ensure that no doors were closed. If we decided we wanted to have another child, we might be able to because of the genetic testing. The biopsies were the only chance to determine it.

It felt selfish to say yes. In my heart, I just wanted Ryken left alone. All the blood tests and needles seemed inconsequential now that he was dying. We did not have time to ponder; the doctors needed an answer immediately.

I asked if the biopsies would hurt him, and I was told they would not. He was given pain medication. We trusted Dr. Uchi even though we had just met him. He was a special person, and I knew that we were sent to the neonatal unit instead of the pediatric unit because Dr. Uchi was supposed to be Ryken's doctor. Brett and I agreed to the biopsies and signed the consent forms.

It was scheduled for three o'clock, before Ryken was taken off of life support. We were supposed to trust our doctors—and everyone else who was trying to help us— since they were the experts. We were barely functioning due to all the information and stress. I went back to see Ryken. I was carrying the heavy knowledge that soon he wouldn't be there to kiss and touch.

After a few moments, I pumped my milk to alleviate the pain and engorgement in my breasts. I was numb. I saw a beautiful poem on the wall. It was titled, "A Special Child," and the author was unknown.

A meeting was held quite far from earth!
It's time again for another birth.
The angels said to the Lord above,
This special child will need much love.
He will require some extra care,

From the folds he meets on the earth down there.
He may not run, or laugh or play,
But he will be loved more and more each day.
So let's be careful where he's sent.
We want his life to be content.
Please, Lord, find the parents who will do this
special job for you.
They will not realize right away the difficult
role they're asked to play,
But with this child sent from above,
Comes strength, new faith, and richer love.
Soon they will know the privilege given in
caring for their gift from heaven.
Their precious charge so meek and mild is
heaven's very special child.

I finally broke down. I was alone with myself and God. I was unable to hold it in anymore. I was only human. I was only a mother. My tender heart was bleeding to death.

God did not answer my prayers for a miracle. I silently sobbed as my whole body shook with the pain and anxiety I had held within for so long. It had been difficult trying to be brave and strong. I felt my body calming down after this release, and I went back to being numb again.

After I could cry no more, I decided the poem would be good for Ryken's funeral. I was beginning to have conversations in my head. I felt like I was going crazy. Maybe I was crazy. I did not know. I did not care. I really didn't have the time to care one way or the other because my baby was going to be taken off of life support in the next hour. I was sure any mother in my position would feel crazy too. That thought brought me little comfort.

A nurse was kind enough to photocopy the poem for me. I returned to the family room and shared it with everyone. A nurse informed us that Ryken's biopsies had been completed. We went immediately to the NIC unit.

We washed our hands, walked over to Ryken, and peered down at our baby. He was sleeping peacefully. We were allowed to bathe Ryken and dress him for the last time. As I prepared him for the sponge bath, I saw the bandages where the biopsies had been done on his thigh. I felt so selfish for choosing to have the biopsies done. I began to cry again, and my ego berated me for being so selfish. "I am so sorry, Ryken!" I gently washed him for the last time as our families watched us.

It felt surreal that it would be the last time I would wash Ryken's body. As I gently dressed him, trying not to disturb his slumber, I whispered, "I love you." I kissed his cheeks, not fully comprehending that it would all come to an end. My mind was not able to cope with that idea yet.

I was hit with the reality that Ryken might be our last baby—and he was about to die. We might not be having any more children. There was no guarantee that they would find anything in Ryken's genetic makeup. I felt panic and anxiety. I tried to remain calm and push down the feelings and emotions.

I focused on talking quietly to Ryken. I focused on washing and drying him off gently. I changed his diaper and dressed him. Brett was always beside me; his support never faltered.

I said a prayer of gratitude for the molds of Ryken's hands and feet. When Ryken was gone, I would be able to stroke and touch his hands and feet whenever I wanted. It was not a substitute for him, but I was beginning to face that harsh reality.

Waves of nausea rolled over me, enveloping my nervous system, my stomach, my chest, and my throat. It was hard to breathe, but I willed away the panic, fear, and sadness at the idea of Ryken being gone. Nothing would be left but the molds of his hands and feet. I must watch over that precious clay and never break it.

I was unable to comprehend life without Ryken. If I thought about it, I would lose any sense of composure.

CHAPTER 22

Time Is Ticking Away

A s the end of the afternoon drew near, Ryken's time on life support was about to end. We were all around his bassinet. When the machines were removed, it was 4:44. I could feel angels with us in this moment. Helping Ryken and all of us deal with what was happening in our lives at the present. I could feel their love and support for all of us right now as the machines were removed.

Ryken had been taken off of all the machines except for the morphine drip. I was unaware of how much time we would have with him in the family room. Minutes or hours? Maybe just today and through the night? The only thing I could focus on was how gentle the doctor was with my baby. Dr. Uchi picked him up from the bassinet and was cradling him in his arms. He quietly turned to leave the space that had been Ryken's home for the past day and a half. That was where we decided his fate for him. That was where he was baptized. That was where many tears were shed as we all said our good-byes to him.

Dr. Uchi stepped slowly and quietly through NICU as the nurses watched us leave. I was sure they were aware of what was happening. Ryken's time with the machines was up. His body would not function without them, and that was not living. That was not having any quality of life.

Allowing him to remain on the machines would be selfish of us. As much as I did not want to face reality, I had always been a realist. It was simply "not living" to be hooked up to machines with no positive outcome in the future.

The other parents in NICU were oblivious to what was happening. They were focused on their own bundles of joy in the bassinets. They were sending all their prayers and love to their babies, willing them to recover and get well. Wishing for a miracle. That their babies would recover and live. To bring their babies home with them someday. I wished them luck. I hoped their luck was better than my luck had been lately.

I was swiftly jolted back to reality. My reality was that Ryken would not be coming home. Not today—not ever. The nausea and anxiety returned, enveloping me as I walked. I walked beside Brett, holding his hand. Dr. Uchi carried Ryken in front of us.

I focused on Dr. Uchi and our precious baby. He gently carried Ryken out of NICU with an oxygen mask on Ryken's mouth and nose.

We followed them down the long corridor, everyone trailing behind us. It was as though the funeral procession had already begun. I guess it had. This was the last chapter in Ryken's journey on earth.

We walked back to the family room so we could be with Ryken until the end. My baby was going to take his last breath in that room. I had renamed it "Ryken's Room" in my mind.

The door was opened, and all of us filed in. In that space, my baby would only feel love until he saw the light from God and left us to return home to heaven. In that place, we could remain with our baby until he took his last breath. The air was thick with unspoken emotion.

The children's hospital allowed us to remain with Ryken for every step of the way. We would not be asked to leave him alone at night. I would not have to be away from him again.

I felt so much gratitude for Ryken's Room. I was so grateful for the space, which had everything we needed. The room was perfect for us. Being with Ryken for every moment at this stage of the game was a priceless gift for all of us.

As his mom, I could not separate from him yet. I was not ready to let him go. It would have really put me over the edge if I'd had to leave him then. I was barely hanging on. I did not know how much longer I had with "my champion".

Dr. Uchi placed Ryken in Brett's arms after we arranged ourselves on the loveseat. It actually felt normal to sit there and wait for the final moments of Ryken's life to take place. I didn't think it hit me that Ryken would be gone soon. I had no idea what to expect or how much time we had. Dr. Uchi was clear that he did not know how much longer we had with him. No one could give us a time frame. We would just have to wait, live in the moment and take some pictures. We would hold our baby until he decided to leave this world.

That sacred space had everything we needed. The bathroom was just outside the room. It felt far when you were worried your baby was going to pass away while you went to the bathroom. Soiling yourself was not an option— even when you were on a bedside vigil for your baby.

We settled down for the evening. Since I had been nursing Ryken until four days earlier, I was still producing lots of milk. I was pumping every few hours and storing it in the freezer. That would have to stop. I began pumping a little bit of milk from each breast, every few hours, to reduce the pain and the milk production. My breasts were hard, painful, and engorged.

One of the nurses suggested using cabbage leaves as a natural way to stop the milk production. She also gave me some Tylenol. My parents went to the grocery store for a head of cabbage. I put cabbage leaves in my bra and replaced them every few hours with crisp ones. It was a miracle solution. It helped alleviate the pain. Everyone was so kind and helpful. I couldn't imagine what they were thinking, and I did not ask.

I felt like I was living in a twilight zone. I was focused on holding Ryken, sponge-bathing him, and changing his diaper.

Ryken was not given any nutrition, and there was not a lot of pee in the diapers, but it was a way of doing something for him. It was about caring and loving Ryken in his final hours. I kept myself busy by making sure Ryken was comfortable. I touched our noses together and gave him Eskimo kisses. I whispered in his ear over and over to him that I loved him. He never opened his eyes, but I knew he could hear me.

One thing that really bothered me was that Kaden was away from us. He would not have a chance to say good-bye to his baby brother. Brett made a phone call and luckily Brett's brother was able to fly with Kaden to the city we were in. They would stay with Brett's parents at the Ronald McDonald House. I had seen their logo everywhere over the years, but I never thought I would be utilizing their services. I was grateful for such a beautiful haven for my toddler. I said a prayer that Ryken would still be alive when Kaden arrived the following evening.

His aunty and uncle were taking such good care of Kaden. We had no worries about him; his big cousins were his favorite people in the world. Brett and I just wanted our family together for the little time that we had left. My stepdad offered to pick them up at the airport and drive them to the hospital. All the help and support was great, and we needed it.

Brett and I could not wait for Kaden to be with us. Knowing that we were losing Ryken made our need to have Kaden with us even stronger. I wanted to sit and rock Ryken until he left this world that I had to remain in. A world without him in it.

Other people wanted to come to the hospital but I was not prepared to share Ryken with anyone else. I was finally learning boundaries and what was important for me. Brett, our parents, our siblings, my best friend, and I took turns holding and rocking Ryken.

I willed Ryken not to die during this time. It killed me on the inside to share him, but I knew Ryken was God's child as well as mine.

"Ryken was their grandson."

"Ryken was their nephew."

"They should get to hold him too."

"He was not just mine and Brett's baby."

Our family stayed for a few hours. We quietly cried and visited. The doctor and nurse checked on Ryken numerous times, listening to his lungs and heart. They asked in compassionate voices if we needed anything.

Actually I need a miracle. I never allowed those words to slip past my tongue. Instead I would reply, "No, we are doing well."

My brain started connecting the dots. There would be no miracle. My new miracle was time with Ryken in this room.

Just before midnight, Brett went into NICU and retrieved the replica of Ryken's little hands and feet. It matched him perfectly—even his little bent toe. I was so worried about that little toe affecting how he would walk. It did not matter anymore. He wouldn't ever be learning how to walk.

I felt the sadness rising up again. I pushed it down. I focused on the clay molds. I was able to put my finger inside Ryken's left hand as if he were holding onto my finger. I could feel Ryken's palm and stroke the inside of his hand and fingers. I would always treasure this work of art. Our wonderful nurse had given us a priceless gift. I was full of gratitude for the little things. They kept the pain of what was actually going on at bay—for the time being.

We got ready for bed shortly after midnight. Brett and I went to the washroom separately. Each of us had been terrified that Ryken would pass away while we were brushing our teeth. We settled in for the night: Brett was by the wall, Ryken was in the middle, and I was on the outside, closest to the window.

The moonlight cast a beautiful glow in the room. I felt peaceful, which was nice after all the other emotions I was going through. We fell asleep, not knowing what the night would bring. We did not know if Ryken would be with us in the morning. Sleep found us, and we welcomed it with open arms.

There were no issues during the night. We all slept well. Ryken never made a sound, and surprisingly I did not wake up to check on him.

At seven o'clock, the nurse came in to check on Ryken. His breathing was shallow, and he was pale. He looked comfortable, and his skin was warm. Ryken had been opening up his eyes occasionally. She encouraged us to call NICU with any questions or concerns. I was grateful for her kindness.

At eight o'clock, my sisters and my parents brought coffee and muffins for us. God bless them. Since I was not nursing anymore, I was drinking coffee and having dairy again. As I sipped the warm drink, I thought, *I would give all of it up forever if I could have Ryken forever.* I tried to stay present. I ate and drank while silently reminding myself of the harsh reality I was living in at the moment. The next reality I would be facing was Ryken's death.

We chatted quietly about our uneventful night. I asked my mom and sisters to go shopping for a few outfits for Ryken since he had no clothes. They seemed anxious to help and went out on their mission.

They came back a few hours later with the cutest and most comfortable outfits. They also found a beautiful, soft blue blanket. It was embroidered with three symbols and three letters. There was an airplane for the letter A, a butterfly for the letter B, and a car for the letter C.

I softly touched the blanket and said, "Ryken drove in a car to come home. He flew in an airplane to get here. And soon, he will fly with the butterflies to heaven." I began to weep with the magnitude of my words. My body shook with the intensity of the sadness I had been carrying. The pain tore down the walls I had built as I tried to be strong.

The words entered my brain and left my mouth without time to think. My mom and sisters began to cry as well. I wrapped my baby in his new blanket and gently rocked him in the green recliner. Tears continued to flow silently down my cheek as I gave Ryken Eskimo kisses. The minutes ticked on as we each struggled with our own pain. We tried to keep our brave faces on.

That afternoon, the doctor observed Ryken. He said Ryken could be transferred back to our home hospital for palliative care if we wished. I wanted to remain there. All of us together in that room. That was a gift for our family. I was concerned that Ryken would die on the way back to our home hospital. Also there was no children's hospital where we lived.

I knew what care Ryken would get here at this children's hospital. I knew we would be allowed to be involved in every step of the process. I did not want anyone helping us with Ryken except Dr. Uchi and his staff.

If we went home, there would be no guarantees for us. I was still reeling from being separated from Ryken for six hours when he was in the intensive care unit. Here, I was guaranteed that we would be allowed to be with him every moment. We would hold him until he took his last breath. No one would separate us. For my own mental health and well-being, I told Dr. Uchi that I would like to remain in Ryken's Room until the end under his supervision.

Brett and I were in sync, and I was grateful. Brett agreed with me, especially since Kaden would arrive soon. He wanted to stay as well. I breathed a huge sigh of relief when Dr. Uchi told us that it would be fine to remain where we were.

We discussed an autopsy and a brain analysis. It was decided that there was no need for either of the procedures. Dr. Uchi agreed with us and respected our wishes.

Ryken opened his eyes, but they were not focused. His color was waxing and waning. The doctor authorized palliative care to begin.

Later that afternoon, Kassandra came back for her shift. She had arranged her work schedule so she would be Ryken's night nurse for the next few days. She was scheduled to be off, but she had changed her shifts to be with Ryken. I knew that she had her own nine-year-old daughter at home, yet she felt compelled to do this. I stared at her in wonder and gave her a hug. I thanked her for being so good with Ryken and kind to us.

She handed me a bag. She had been to the mall between her shifts and had come across a gift. She said, "I just had to buy this for Ryken."

I reached inside and pulled the cutest stuffed giraffe out of the bag.

Kassandra said, "It was his hair. It reminded me of Ryken, and I just had to get it for him. It has a Mohawk just like Ryken does."

I could see what she meant, and we laughed together. I thanked her and gave her a hug. I told Ryken about his new stuffy. I talked to him as if he heard me—as though everything was normal. He had not received many gifts in his short time on earth. This giraffe was so special for us. Kassandra's thoughtful gesture brought some peace to my broken heart. We have named this new giraffe "Kass."

Do I keep the giraffe or bury it with Ryken?

I was having a war in my head. I would have liked it as a reminder, but a voice in my head said, "It's not your giraffe. It's Ryken's. His nurse got it for him. It should go with him." I willed myself back to the present moment.

I placed the giraffe beside Ryken. My beautiful baby was snuggled in the crook of Brett's elbow. His eyes were closed to the world around him.

I started taking pictures, knowing they were the last pictures I would have of him. I shoved that thought away and focused on how sweet my baby was with his stuffed animals. My stepdad had bought some teddy bears that day. One was a baby blue teddy with a baseball. The other was a brown bear with a basketball. One was meant for Kaden when he arrived. I would give Kaden the brown teddy bear and leave the blue one for Ryken. Blue seemed to be Ryken's color.

That evening there was a knock on our door. Kaden! Oh, how I had missed him! I felt tears in my eyes and relief fill my body that Kaden had finally arrived. He was safe and sound after riding on the airplane. My beautiful boy came over for hugs and kisses. No matter how cloudy the day was for me, he was a ray of sunshine in my life.

Brett's brother had forgotten to bring a pull-up with him. Kaden was wearing pants with no underwear or a pull-up. We all laughed, which just goes to show that some things in life are really not a big deal. Kaden had no accidents. I hoped there was something for him at the Ronald McDonald House.

We all adored Kaden. I asked someone to take some pictures. We still did not know how much time we had with Ryken.

I smiled like a fool and kissed Ryken's cheek. I thanked him for waiting for Kaden to arrive and for allowing the pictures to take place. The light had gone out of Brett's eyes, and he was unable to smile for any of the pictures.

The pictures showed a smiling mom, a sad and somber dad, a goofy two-year-old boy, and a beautiful sleeping baby. That was my family. I didn't care. The four of us were together at last. My life was better since Kaden was with us. I felt as though I could breathe a bit easier.

Kaden took the stethoscope and listened to Ryken. It was amazing that they wouldn't grow up together. Ryken opened his eyes when he heard Kaden's voice. The brothers had a soul-to-soul moment. Kaden looked directly into Ryken's eyes, said, "Love you, Ryken," and kissed him. Kaden did not understand what was going on or what the future would hold for him. He would no longer be able to kiss his baby brother and tell him that he loved him when he was gone. There would be no more "peeking" in the bassinet on his baby.

Kaden was living in the moment as children do. He was happy and excited and going with the flow of life. We explained that he got to have a sleepover at the Ronald McDonald House with Grandma and Grandpa. He showed no concerns. He was compliant and happy, which eased my stress. He did not cry or throw a tantrum.

Thank you, Kaden, for being so special. Thank you, Kaden, for not having NKH.

Kaden visited for a few hours before he went on his adventure. I wondered if Kaden would remember any of these moments when he got older.

Brett and I prepared Ryken for sleep. We changed his diaper and made sure he was comfortable. We kissed him good night after I exchanged wilted cabbage leaves for crisp ones. Ryken slept peacefully between us. We were thankful for the morphine he was receiving; we didn't want Ryken to endure any pain.

My family showed up the following morning with coffee and muffins. My mom brought me a tiny silver butterfly encrusted in diamonds on the most delicate silver chain. I began to cry and thanked her. It was beautiful, and I put it on. It would always remind me of Ryken. I would keep it close to my heart forever, but I would have traded anything to have Ryken forever instead.

Later that morning, Dara arrived for an unexpected visit. She lived in the city and brought her nine-month-old daughter. We hugged each other and cried. She brought banana bread, and I cut it up for all of us to eat. I showed off Ryken and held her daughter for the first time. Dara did not know what to do, but she felt like she should come see us. I understood how people wanted to help us. We took more pictures with our children.

She stayed for an hour, and it was a great visit. I was grateful that she got to meet Ryken. If she had called and asked to come, I would have told her no. Maybe it was supposed to be. I was unable to attend her wedding in 2003 because Kaden was only a few weeks old. I had mastitis and was not able to make the six-hour drive. I wished all I had to worry about now was having mastitis. I should have gone to her wedding and realized that my mastitis would be fine. In life, we live and learn.

Later that evening, the nurse checked on Ryken. He was less active, was not opening his eyes as frequently, and his breathing was more shallow. His skin was a lot paler. The metabolics team needed more blood for tests. We give permission for more blood work to be taken through Ryken's central line, which had been inserted in his groin area. It was a way to get blood without poking and prodding him. I was unsure how many needles Ryken had endured so far in his young life, but I knew I couldn't count that high. It was all for his well-being, but it was hard to watch.

It was feeling like Groundhog Day. We went to sleep and woke up with our baby sleeping beside us. Our family and Kaden showed up for visits.

On Tuesday, December 6, Doctor Uchi and the nurse reassessed Ryken. His breathing was irregular, and there were long pauses in between. Dr. Uchi told us he had bad news. The skin and muscle biopsies had not been processed appropriately. They would not be able to be sent away for genetic testing. Metabolics requested repeat tests on Ryken.

The doctor was quite upset. He had spoken personally with the individual who had not stored them properly. He asked us if we wanted to have the person apologize to us. Brett and I said it was not necessary.

I could tell by our doctor's words and his facial expression that the person was talked to in earnest. I felt an anxiety attack coming on. I was not prepared for it. I did not want Ryken to die on the procedure table during a second round of biopsy procedures. I shared my concern with the doctor.

Dr. Uchi discussed how the biopsy testing could be completed postmortem. After Ryken passed away, they would have the surgeon repeat the procedures. He was giving us his personal guarantee that the next biopsies would be stored properly and would be viable.

I was hit full force again with the reality that Ryken was going to die eventually. I felt the heaviness in my chest. Inside Ryken's Room, I had built a sanctuary with my baby and our family. It was hard to hear the words *postmortem*. Even though a part of my brain knew we were waiting for Ryken to die, my heart continued to love in denial. I was soaking up every moment with Ryken. I was unable to imagine a life without him.

I convinced my brain to focus.

We agreed to have the surgeon repeat the biopsies postmortem. It was our only possibility of having another child together.

Dr. Uchi apologized again profusely.

The doctors and nurses were such kind and humble people. I felt blessed to have a medical team that cared so much about Ryken and our family.

CHAPTER 23

The End Is Near

I was living in my own dreamland. I had left my own reality to venture into this world where only love exists and time was slipping away. I was on a mission of taking as many pictures and making as many memories as possible with Ryken, along with our family.

I had an idea that I needed a picture of our family by the Christmas tree. We also needed to go for a walk. We placed Ryken in the buggy with his morphine drip, gathered up Kaden, and walked to the elevator.

My anxiety was manageable on our outing. We were walking around like a "normal" family. This in itself was ridiculous to me, but we were doing it anyway. I wanted that picture taken.

We found a Christmas tree and took pictures beside it with Kaden and Ryken. It was amazing, but it also felt normal. I would never have another opportunity for a family picture with Ryken and Kaden beside a Christmas tree. All I could think of was getting as many pictures as I could with the four of us as a family. It was our family, and it was what our "normal" looked like. I would have regretted not taking the pictures.

This is your only opportunity to have a family Christmas picture with your boys.

If I stopped to give my future some thought, I would break down. The harsh reality was that Ryken would not be around next Christmas. For that matter, he would not be around this Christmas. That thought echoed in the hollows of my mind, like taunting shadows, dancing to the beat of their own drum. I pushed the shadows away and focused on trying to smile for the camera.

We walked to Ryken's room, and it felt good to stretch my legs. I looked down at my precious baby and felt a powerful wave of emotion. It would be the last time I pushed him in a stroller. The last time he got to go for a ride. My heart began to ache, and my throat had a lump in it. I willed it away and denied the truth that would soon be my reality. *Ryken is still here, and I can give him a little ride in his buggy.*

We hugged our little monkey, and Kaden headed back to the Ronald McDonald House. I called my astrologer friend who had helped us plan the time and date for our wedding. I asked if he could do Ryken's chart for me. I gave him Ryken's time and date of birth. In the reading, he gave me some interesting information.

Ryken had five lines going through his career house. Typically a person has only two or three lines in that area. Ryken's career was to be a "teacher." I got goose bumps when I heard those words. My son was born to be a teacher. The news warmed my heart, and I felt as though I knew Ryken even better.

I thanked my friend and hung up the phone. As we got ready for bed, I told Brett about Ryken's chart. I peered down at our son, smiled at him, and said, "So, you are a teacher, my precious boy."

That information really helped me. For some strange reason, I felt a sense of pride about "Ryken the teacher." I was unsure exactly what it meant, but it was enough to feel that comfort for now. "Good night, my little professor. May our angels bless each of us with a good rest." I shut off the lights, and the three of us drifted off to sleep.

The next morning was no different than our past seven mornings. My parents and my sister brought us coffee and muffins. I was pumping less, and my milk was drying up. The cabbage leaves continued to be helpful. Shortly before lunch, Brett's parents and Kaden arrived. We were all in a great mood, considering the circumstances. I was even able to allow people to laugh in the room without glaring at them. It had been a week of living like that and I was mellowing I guess.

At noon, I decided we should go down to the cafeteria with Ryken to have lunch with everyone. It would be good to go down to the cafeteria to order some different food. I also thought it would be fun to be with Kaden and everyone else as well. I pushed Ryken in his buggy, and Kaden pressed the elevator button. Joy in simple things. We walked into the cafeteria, ordered some food, and ate together.

Midway through my lunch, I had an awful feeling in my stomach and my throat began to hurt. I looked at Brett and said, "We have to go back to Ryken's room. Right now." I needed to leave. It hurt to breathe, and I felt anxiety take hold of my chest. I hurriedly gathered my things and left the unfinished food on the tray.

I started pushing the buggy through the cafeteria. I was having a full blown anxiety attack. I was overcome with a dreadful feeling that Ryken was going to die in the carriage. It took all my control not to bolt past everyone to get back to the room.

I walked as fast as I could without running and hurting anyone. *Dear God, please don't let Ryken die in this buggy. Please don't let Ryken die in this buggy.* He was still sleeping peacefully, but something inside me told me I needed to hurry.

In the elevator, I looked down at my baby and prayed he was okay. *I am so angry about going to that stupid cafeteria. What was I thinking? Let's just go off for lunch like a normal family on a little picnic in the cafeteria. Like we are the Brady Bunch or something. We are anything but normal.*

We are waiting for our baby to die. To take his last breath. My life had gone from picture perfect to a painful and emotional roller-coaster ride from hell.

We got off the elevator, opened the door, and entered Ryken's Room. I looked down into the buggy. Ryken's whole face had started turning blue. I carefully grabbed him out of the carriage. I was shaking, trembling with fear that he had died. "Ryken ... Ryken ... Ryken." My voice was high pitched and unrecognizable. "Don't leave me. Don't leave me, Ryken."

Ryken took a breath, and his face turned pink again. I snuggled him close to my heart and gave him Eskimo kisses. Tears spilled down my face and landed on his beautiful skin. "You're okay. You have not left me yet. You did not die in the carriage. Thank you, God. Thank you, Ryken."

Brett called into NICU to let them know what was happening. Dr. Uchi and a different nurse came to see him right away. It was Sunday, December 11. We asked our family to leave as it felt like the end was near.

We said good-bye to Kaden, told him we loved him, planted kisses all over him, as we hugged him good-bye. He was happy to leave with his grandma and grandpa since the Ronald McDonald House had so many toys and things to do.

The nurse and doctor had no answers regarding how long Ryken had left, except to tell us this was one of the last stages before the body stopped. I had been running from reality for a week. I had built a new reality in my mind. I had been living in the façade that Ryken's Room was our new home. I did not think it would ever end.

Over the next three or four hours, Ryken's face turned a bluish-purple. He would stop breathing for half a minute or longer. Even though it was probably only twenty or thirty seconds, it felt like an eternity to me. Every time we thought Ryken had died, he would take another breath. His face would slowly return to a normal color, and he would blow air out at us.

A few minutes later, he started to turn blue and purple again. Then he would take another breath. The most bizarre part was the feeling that Ryken was scaring us. We watched him closely, peering down at his face, waiting on pins and needles and thinking he had passed away. We were full of fear that he was gone. Ryken would take another big gasp of air and look normal again.

For a few hours, I sat beside Brett while he held Ryken. I could never forget how strong Brett was for Ryken and me. It was the most difficult and painful part of the journey.

It was also a real turning point for me. Even though I kept telling Ryken every night that he could fly to heaven with the butterflies, I was not ready to let him go. The words did not reflect what my heart felt. My heart was still not prepared to say good-bye. Every night, I told him that he did not have to stay for us—and I thought I meant it. I realize now that I hadn't.

I could not imagine life outside of that room. I could not imagine life without Ryken. I knew he turned purple for those hours so I could let him go. He did it to get my heart to release my hold on him. My heart had staked a claim to keep my baby with me, but watching him turn purple helped my heart release him as best as I could. Even though I thought that I had been letting him go, I really hadn't. I knew it was time. I was finally ready to let Ryken go. Watching him suffer with his breathing made me realize it.

What was left of my shattered heart said, "It's time to go, Ryken. I can let you go now." This time I meant every word that I had just whispered in his ear.

I felt myself shifting inside. I did not feel like the same person. I felt hollow and empty. I told myself that I would never be the same person again. I barely recognized who I was or what life was about. Every moment felt like an eternity. I was unable to prevent the tears from falling.

They were connected to my heart, and the pain had to go somewhere.

After four hours, he stopped turning blue and purple. He decided to open his eyes for thirty minutes. It was the most amazing gift. I held him and stared into his beautiful blue eyes. He returned my gaze. I spoke softly about how much I loved him and bestowed a thousand Eskimo kisses on his delicate little nose. I could feel our souls intertwining on a much deeper level than just a mother and her baby. Ryken and I were connected beyond these moments together. These moments will be branded into my memory. Ryken was still with me. These moments with him are full of peace and love.

The waiting game was still on, but something shifted in me. I was ready to face the truth. Death was imminent. It would be coming and knocking on our door and asking for Ryken. It was my job as Ryken's mom to be prepared to answer it with dignity and grace. I was finally ready to open the door and face death. Ryken's death.

Brett and I got ready for bed and tucked Ryken in between us. We kissed him, and I knew that he might not be awake in the morning. With a heavy heart, I wiped away my tears and closed my eyes. I prayed to God for strength while I slept. I prayed that in the morning I would be strong, full of strength for the difficult days ahead of me. I knew my life in Ryken's Room was about to come to an end.

CHAPTER 24

Ascension to Heaven

The morning of December 12 started like the eight previous mornings. Brett and I shared a good morning kiss before descending our love upon Ryken. We gave him kisses, and Brett and I chatted about how well we had slept. Ryken never stirred or woke up during the night.

When Dr. Uchi arrived, our family went into the hallway to give us some privacy. I rested my hand on Ryken's legs as we chatted.

Dr. Uchi knelt down beside the bed and placed the stethoscope on Ryken's chest. He looked up at us with a quiet sadness on his face and said, "I am sorry. Ryken has passed." He moved the stethoscope around and checked again for the heartbeat. We were right there, and we missed him taking his last breath. Just like that, Ryken was gone.

I looked at the alarm clock: 9:33. We were beside him for every moment during the last eight days, and he left the world when we weren't looking. He was gone. His heart no longer beat with any rhythm. There was no breath left in his lungs.

I knelt down beside my baby and looked into his face. The pain inside was so deep that no amount of anything could fill it. The doctor talked about the biopsy being done right away. *In my mind I hear, yes, he has to go now for a moment. He will be right back though.* He called NICU from our room to make the arrangements.

A nurse came to the room, gathered up my baby and took him for the second muscle biopsy. There was a guilt growing in me about having the biopsies done again. I tried to shove it away and remember the advice from the genetic doctor and counselors. If we wanted to keep the door open to have children in the future, it was an important step.

I tried to trust in something that I didn't even know if I still believed: faith in a power greater than me. Watching Ryken die had shaken me up. I was unsure of what life was all about now. I felt waves of numbness wash over me. I reminded myself that they would bring Ryken back to me soon. After my shower, I would get to hold him and say good-bye again.

I softly cried in despair and disbelief that he was actually gone. Our time with him had come to an end. Life in this room was over. I felt numb. I was empty and hollow inside. Darkness took over my mind. No words were going to ease the sorrow or fix my pain. The reality was settling in quickly.

Our family offered their condolences, but it did not seem real. They would remain in Ryken's Room while we showered. They would bring Ryken back after the surgeon completed the procedures and we would be there for him.

I gathered myself and stepped out of the family room. It had been my cocoon and safe haven for eight days. I was free to leave, but I did not want to. I just wanted my baby back. I just wanted to hold Ryken again and stay in the confines of that room.

I was the only person in the hall as I walked to the shower. It felt odd to be outside that room. I felt completely and utterly alone. I had no more baby. No more Ryken. My world seemed odd, and I felt completely disassociated from it. I walked down the hall in a fog.

I did not enjoy the rush of warmth that I usually feel when I shower. I was not grateful for a shower even though

I had not showered for eleven days. All I could think of was Ryken. There were no tears. I just felt numb in every part of my body.

The thoughts in my head were playing like a broken record. *My baby is gone. My baby is gone. My baby is gone. What am I going to do without Ryken? What am I going to do without Ryken? What am I going to do without Ryken? My baby is gone!*

What should have been the best shower of my life were the worst moments of my life. The hot water hit my skin, and all I could think about was how I was going to live without my baby, my beautiful Ryken. It was the beginning of my separation from my beloved son, and the pain already hurt too much.

When I got back to the family room, a nurse brought Ryken to us. Brett and I took turns holding him. He looked so peaceful, like a doll. There was no more swelling. His beautiful face was full of peace and serenity. Even in death, Ryken had the face of an angel. It was hard to take my eyes off of his sweet face. His grandmas held him too. He was rocked over and over with love in the rocker recliner. Kaden came for a visit as well. Tears were shed, but no words were going to bring me solace or comfort.

The funeral arrangements had to be made. We were seven hours from home. I wondered what to do next. The nurses were helpful beyond anything I could have wished for. They asked us which funeral home we would use and made the call for us. The funeral home would drive out to get Ryken. My anxiety magnified at the thought of leaving him with a stranger for the drive home. I said, "No. I am not leaving the hospital without my baby."

As luck would have it, our nurse shared a story about a family from a reserve up north. They did not want to leave their baby behind and put their baby in a basket. The baby traveled with them on the plane. Another earth angel was helping us along the way. It was an answered prayer. I said, "Yes, that is what I want us to do."

I thank God that Brett agreed with the plan.

Our nurse left to see what she could do. We chatted, played with Kaden, and surrounded Ryken with love. A few minutes later, the nurse returned with a beautiful rectangular wicker basket and some blankets. We made a soft bed with a blanket for Ryken and placed him in the basket at an angle so he would be comfortable. Even in death, I wanted to protect him.

Grief was closing in on me. A team was working together, and I imagined them saying, "Hey, everyone. We have a new mom waiting in the wings. She just lost her baby. Let's go get her, round her up, give her a few shots of anger and shock, a dollop of denial, and load her up on numbness. This death was a doozy. Send a note to God. He has his work cut out for him."

I tried to focus on the nurse. She covered him up with a white blanket. Ryken looked like a doll as he lay in the basket. For the drive home, they gave us another white blanket to place over the top of the basket. It felt right to me.

We had to wait for the death certificate. Brett and I had refused an autopsy because we did not want Ryken poked and prodded anymore. I did not want his brain cut into. I just needed his poor little body left alone. I wanted Ryken left alone.

At six o'clock, the paperwork was completed and the signed death certificate was placed in our hands. Just like that, we were leaving the safety of the room where we had shared our last precious days as a family. I felt that we were blessed with the miracle of being with Ryken until he took his last breath. This did not alleviate the grief I was feeling though.

Brett carried Ryken's basket to our car with so much care and love. What was left of my heart broke some more as Brett unhooked the car seat so the wicker basket could be buckled in. Like the amazing father Brett is, he buckled in the basket as if it were Ryken's car seat and fastened the seat belt. Our baby was safe and sound for the long drive home.

I walked over to my stepfather's truck. Kaden was buckled into his car seat already. The seat was still there from a week ago when Kaden was picked up at the airport. I jumped in the back and buckled myself in beside him. Brett's dad was in the passenger seat. I gave Kaden a hug and a kiss. My mom and Brett's mom were in our car with Brett and Ryken.

As we began the long drive to the funeral home, I chatted with Kaden. I had missed my precious son so much. I gave him hugs and kisses and held his little hand. Kaden was so soft and warm. He was alive and well—thank God.

I said "Kaden, Ryken is in heaven now."

Kaden started crying and said, "No wings, Mommy, no wings."

I was a bit taken aback. He was telling me that Ryken was getting wings because he was an angel in heaven now. He was telling me in the only way he knew how. He was saying how sad he was that Ryken was an angel now and not here with us.

I sat there in wonder and amazement. It astounded me. I knew Kaden was connected to the other side and knew what was going on. In my heart and soul, I knew that Kaden's tears and comment was his own grief about losing his baby brother. I looked at him in astonishment as my own tears began to fall. I tried to comfort him as best as I could. I was in a state of disbelief. I had never talked with Kaden about angels, wings, heaven, God, or anything else like that.

It was the longest ride of my life. Kaden fell asleep, and I was in so much pain. The two dads chitchatted and listened to the radio, which annoyed me to no end. My life was in utter disarray, and they were acting like nothing had happened. Most men do not know what to say to anyone grieving—let alone an emotional mom on the day her baby died.

I had nothing to say to them, and they had no words to console me. Even if they knew what to say, it would not have helped. *What were my mom and Brett's mom thinking? Why am I here? Why aren't Kaden, Brett, Ryken, and I together? Do they think I would lose it driving back with my dead baby all tucked in his basket and safely strapped in? Do they think Kaden should not see Ryken? He was covered by a white blanket for crying out loud! All I would have said was that Ryken was under the blanket and resting with his angels. I didn't get it!*

Maybe we were in such a hurry to leave that no one put any thought into it. *Grief and stress. That must be it.* I closed my eyes and slept for a bit. It helped—but not nearly enough.

How am I supposed to leave my baby at the funeral home? I am not having him picked and poked at again. I am not having him embalmed either. I just want him left alone!

What are the moms thinking? Why are Kaden and I with the two grandpas? Are they scared of Kaden riding with Ryken now that he is dead? Are people scared of me riding with Ryken now that he is dead?

It's amazing how things happen when you are grieving. I would have liked to have been with my husband, my boys, Kaden, and Ryken. No offense to the dads, but really? I was sure they were wondering how they got stuck with me. I could tell they were uncomfortable. I was uncomfortable too. I wanted to scream in pain and agony, but I did not want to freak Kaden out—or the two grandpas up front. Their job was to deliver me to the final destination. One crazy, grief-stricken, emotional mom needed to get to the funeral home.

Time was ticking slowly, and I stared at my oldest son. Kaden was sleeping soundly. He was so beautiful and sweet. I rested my head beside Kaden and dozed off to escape the nightmare I was living.

We arrived around midnight. I opened the door, and the cold air took my breath away. It was trying to freeze my blood and steal the warmth from my heart. *Too late,* I thought. *That happened sixteen and a half hours ago when Ryken stopped breathing.*

Brett unlatched Ryken's seatbelt, grabbed the basket with care, and made sure Ryken was covered by the blanket.

The funeral people were kind. I had met them a year before when Garret died. They talked calmly and quietly. Leaving Ryken there would be the hardest thing I had ever done. My stomach was in knots, and I wanted to throw up.

A voice in my head said, "Suck it up, buttercup. This is only the beginning."

Kaden was still sleeping in the truck, and he needed me. I felt as though I had disassociated a bit from the events taking place. My heart was hurting, and I felt like I was slowly dying.

I said, "I do not want him embalmed."

They agreed.

My thoughts were running rampant, like a wildfire out of control. I said, "I want my baby left alone. No more needles. No more pokes. No more prods. No more chemicals in his body."

Nothing they could say was going to make it any easier. The separation was beyond difficult. It began with my shower and the second biopsies. I had been separated from Ryken for the entire drive. My living child needed his mom. He had not really had me for eight weeks. That was where my first instinct went. Kaden needed me. I also needed to begin to detach from Ryken.

I do not believe in hell, but I believe there can be hell on earth. I was so numb inside. I wanted to cry and yell, "No! I am not leaving Ryken here! I don't want you to touch him."

I wanted to ask if they would be gentle when they touched him. *Will they move him around like a rag doll with no care or concern for him when they dress him for the funeral? They seem like nice people, but how would I know? I won't know if they hurt him when I leave. How can I leave him here?*

I touched his body and kissed his cheek. I did what I was supposed to do. I left my baby's body in the hands of strangers. Coldness and numbness took hold of my heart. Ice was trying to form around it, but ice can't stick to a broken heart. My heart had been shattered into minuscule broken pieces. Each had razor-sharp edges that dripped and gleamed with agony and pain.

God had not answered my prayers.

We would return the next day to choose a coffin. Cremation was not even discussed. Having Ryken's body burned would make me lose any last shred of sanity I was holding onto. I was hovering at the brink of despair. I was about to fall off the cliff. Having his body cremated would make what was left of my mind step over the edge and fall down into the pits of insanity. I would never be seen or heard from again. I would be nothing but a broken mother at the bottom of it.

A voice in my head repeated, "Kaden needs you now."

I softly kissed my baby good-bye. His spirit was not there. It was just his body, a shell. He looked like a doll—peaceful, calm, beautiful—but he was my baby. Hours ago, he had been my living baby. "I love you, Ryken," I whispered near his ear. *Did he hear me? I don't know.*

I stepped away. I knew the next thing I would choose for his bed would be his coffin. I stepped out into the bitter night. In my mind, I was holding onto the thought of how we would choose a coffin. A piece of me wanted to scream and lash out at the world. I pushed those emotions down and went through the motions. I got in the vehicle and made sure Kaden was buckled up. I closed my eyes for a moment. Life was an abyss of pain and tragedy. I slipped back into the welcoming arms of shock and numbness.

We drove to my parents' farm for the night, and Kaden stayed asleep.

Thank you, God, for Kaden. My sunshine.

CHAPTER 25

Planning Ryken's Funeral

We met with the priest in the small town where I grew up. We were having the funeral in the Catholic Church where I was baptized and took all my sacraments. I had attended many masses, weddings, and funerals here. Brett had said it did not matter to him where we had the funeral.

I took great comfort in having Ryken's funeral in my church. It made me wonder where the funeral would have been if Ryken had been baptized United? I was full of gratitude in that moment that he had been baptized Catholic. I knew it was aligned that way so I could have the funeral in my hometown. I knew why there was a Catholic priest at the hospital. The funeral was for my comfort. Brett told me we would do whatever brought me peace. It did not matter to him. There was no greater peace for me than walking through my hometown church doors and having Ryken's funeral here.

We discussed using Celine Dion's music for the service and prayers. The priest was kind, compassionate, and understanding. We lived in a different community, in a different city, and he had not met either of us before. He said we could use whatever music we needed for the funeral and for prayers. That was a very unusual allowance for a

Catholic Mass, and I again said another quiet prayer of gratitude.

We had to choose readings for the funeral. I had to begin writing the eulogy. We had to get information to the funeral home for the funeral cards as soon as possible. I was overwhelmed and stressed. *I want this to be perfect for Ryken.* Moving slowly and steadily, I completed each task without crying. I had a job to do and luckily I was able to focus.

After meeting with the priest, we went to choose a plot for Ryken. There were three available around Garret. We chose the one just below Garret's grave. I was filled with a feeling of peace for the briefest of moments knowing that Garret and Ryken were together. I slipped back into my robotic stage of numbness to continue working on my "to do" list.

Brett and I drove back to the funeral home. I asked to see Ryken. They went in the back and brought out his basket. I pulled back the white blanket and saw my beautiful baby. I touched his cheek and kissed him. He was so cold. I stroked his little hands and said, "I love you. I love you. I love you."

My heart screamed. I wanted to grab him and hold him close to my heart. I wanted to give him Eskimo kisses, rock him, and sing him a lullaby. Instead, shock kicked in. I covered him with the blanket and thanked the funeral attendant. I was thankful for the gift of seeing and touching my beautiful baby. I reiterated that I did not want him embalmed.

We went to the room where the coffins were displayed. For adults, there were many colors and stains of wood to choose from. There were two coffins for babies. One was light blue, and one was light pink. They were made out of satin, both inside and outside, and were identical except for the color. Pink or blue, which one do you choose? Brett and I hated them. It was like a cruel joke, and we were the stars of a bizarre TV show called "Our Life." It was depressing.

Maybe we should choose the pink one for Ryken to throw everyone off during the funeral. It could be part of the eulogy. *The joke's on you. He really was a boy, but we felt the color pink was a nicer color than the blue.*

The colors seemed to be a twisted joke for grieving parents. *Your baby is not alive but can be forever known by the color of the coffin? Blue for boys or pink for girls. Aren't we lucky?*

I add funeral home attendant to the list of jobs I would never want.

I said, "Do you have anything else?"

He took us to a different room. He showed us a beautiful casket made out of oak. It was stained white, and the inside was beautiful white satin. Brett and I agreed that it was the one we wanted. The blue coffin was free, but we didn't care about the price. We didn't even ask about it. There would be no first bike for Ryken. There would be no first car at sixteen. It would be one of our last purchases for him. The next big purchase would be Ryken's headstone. I tried to stay focused and calm, but a storm was raging on the inside.

We drove to the mall and I helped Brett pick out a black suit, a blue shirt, and a black, blue, and silver striped tie. It was depressing and painful. The reality was hard to grasp that we were shopping for clothes for our baby's funeral because we were so numb.

I found a skirt, a shirt, and an emerald green coat that was very appropriate for Ryken's funeral. I wish it was Ryken's blue, but I didn't have time to be choosy. I got some tall black winter boots that were warm as well. The thought of Ryken in the cold ground, all alone, was going to break what was left of my self-control.

The salespeople asked if I was looking for anything in particular.

Actually, yes, I am. It's for my baby's funeral. He just died on Monday, and I am supposed to find something special to wear. What do you suggest would be a good outfit? I was thinking of something blue. Baby blue to be exact.

Instead, I nodded politely and said, "No, thank you." I continued to look on my own. I was able to find black dress pants and a sweater. I headed to the changing room and tried them on. As I headed to the counter to pay, a winter scarf called my name. It was white, gray, dark blue, and Ryken's color of blue. I decided to wear something blue in honor of him.

I wrote the eulogy on the drive home. Brett's cell phone was ringing and it was 10 pm. The funeral home was calling to say Ryken's body was deteriorating quickly. If I wanted to see him over the next few days—and on the day of the funeral—they would need to embalm him.

I said, "If we choose not to embalm Ryken, then what?"

They would not recommend viewing the body again because it would have deteriorated too much. The idea of not seeing Ryken again when I had only three more days to visit him was insane.

They would not have to cut into his body. Ryken's medication line in his right hip was easily accessible, and they would use that area.

Brett and I told them to go ahead with the embalming process. I thanked them for the call. I thanked God that Brett and I felt the same way. It would have killed me to not see Ryken again.

Our house was quiet and looked just as we had left it two weeks earlier. I walked into our living room and touched Ryken's bassinet. I went to Ryken's room and turned on the light. I saw his crib, his bedding, and his teddy bear mobile. I turned the knob and listened to the sound of the mobile as it turned round and round above the crib. There was no more baby to go with it though. There was no more Ryken. Tears began to form in my eyes and fell down my cheeks. I willed the pain away. There was still so much to do.

I scanned the room and thought about what belongings I would bring for the funeral. I put Ryken's brown slippers on the dresser to bring with me. I would deal with the rest after I slept.

I was so thankful to have Brett with me as we went through this. We went to bed, and I was grateful that my mind and body allowed me to slip into a deep sleep each night. It was my only escape from what was happening.

Good night, Kaden. Good night Ryken. I love you both. I close my eyes and drift away.

In the morning, we decided to use Kaden's baptismal outfit for Ryken. It would fit him, and it would be something of his older brother's that he could have. It was the last thing Kaden could pass down to his baby brother.

We drove back to the funeral chapel to see Ryken. He looked as peaceful, and beautiful as the day he was born. I said a silent prayer that the sanity of my higher self gave permission to have him embalmed. I was thankful he was not cremated. I kissed his face and touched his cheek.

Brett and I discussed which pictures to leave with him. I added some pictures to the coffin for Ryken and some of his stuffies. The giraffe from his night nurse was placed closest to him.

My grandfather and his sister came in to pay their respects. They hugged me and peered down at Ryken in his coffin. It was not how I would have liked to show him off to them, but beggars can't be choosers. Sadness and anger danced together inside me as the tears fell from my eyes like raindrops.

My great-aunty said, "He is so cute."

I said, "I know, isn't he?"

She put her arm around me, and I was comforted by their gesture of taking the time to come see Ryken. She told me that she was so sorry that we lost him. She had lost one of her grown daughters to an autoimmune disease a few years earlier and understood my pain.

We gushed over my baby. I was angry at the turn of events that had taken place, but there was no time for anger. I still had a lot of work to do and a eulogy to finish writing.

That afternoon, I had a phone chat with my youngest sister. Mindy told me that she and Deann had gone to the funeral home to see Ryken during their lunch hour.

I said, "That was nice of you. How was Ryken looking?"

Mindy said, "Good. At first, I felt awkward holding him, but it felt normal after a few minutes."

"What?" I didn't think I'd heard her right. "You picked Ryken up and held him?"

Mindy replied, "Deann grabbed him out of the wicker basket and held him. She told me you would want us to hold him. She passed him over to me. I was a bit shocked at first, but after a few minutes, it felt normal."

"You both held him?"

"Yes, we did. We were there for almost an hour."

Deann was in her first year of teaching and had gone to see Ryken during her lunch break. She called Mindy and asked her to meet at the funeral home for a lunch date with Ryken.

I love my sisters. With tears falling down my cheek, I said, "Thank you for doing that." I was shocked by the kindness of my sweet sisters.

I could not hold Ryken. I was fearful that if I picked him up and held him close to my heart, I would not be able to put him back down. Deep inside my soul, I knew I could never hold him again.

Part of me felt like a failure as his mother by admitting that to myself. However, another part of me knew—beyond a shadow of a doubt—that I was fighting the demon of insanity. In order to remain sane and make it through the funeral and burial, I had to take certain precautionary measures.

I could not physically hold Ryken in my arms. If I chose to do that, I would not be able to give Ryken back to the funeral attendants. I would not place him back in the wicker basket. I needed certain boundaries to keep my sanity in check.

Needless to say, I took great comfort that my sisters were able to hold Ryken for me in a time when I could not. Besides Brett, Kaden, and Ryken, the other two people in the world who I would do anything for were those two girls. We were sisters, but my love for them ran deeper than that. We were so connected. It was as if their souls knew I could not step up and do it. They did it for me when I could not. I would be eternally grateful to them.

They had my back when I was so lost. They would snuggle the physical shell of my baby while I was floundering around like a fish out of water, barely able to breathe.

I finished writing the eulogy, and my closest girlfriends met me at my parents' farm. I showed them pictures of Ryken and explained his short life. I was even able to smile and laugh. Each of them took a picture and made a page for the blue memory book that would be viewed at the funeral. Sharing what happened over the past two months helped my heart heal a bit. There was such a desire to tell anyone who would listen about him. My love for Ryken was the same as my love for Kaden—unconditional and overpowering.

As we worked on the memory book, I even laughed at some of my stories about Ryken. It felt good to laugh again, but I felt guilty at the same time.

Brett and Kaden were building an igloo outside. They were bundled up tightly and were having so much fun together. Thank God Kaden has Brett for a dad. It seems like men have to do something with their grief. They process by doing tasks, working on projects, or working. I needed to talk and cry about my grief. I needed to talk and share my memories of Ryken with friends. Though they never got to see Ryken in person or hold him, the memory book was a great way to share his short life with them.

At the prayer service, which was customary for a Catholic funeral, Deann read the book called *Lifetimes:*

Pamela Larocque

The Beautiful Way to Explain Death to Children by Bryan Mellonie and Robert Ingpen. Kassandra gave the book to Kaden at the children's hospital. My sister-in-law read the poem from the hospital, "A Special Child". I did not have to speak.

CHAPTER 26

The Second Worst Day of My Life

I was thankful to have had a good night's sleep as I prepared to face the second worst day of my life. I was able to eat and helped Kaden get ready. I hugged him and realized how lucky I was to have him. I had missed my beautiful boy so much. I kissed him, and he stayed with my family while Brett and I went to the church. We made sure Ryken's picture and his belongings were at the front of the church.

I picked up Ryken's blue puppy and held it to my heart for a moment. I placed it back on the table and was so glad I had kept it for myself. There were many bouquets of flowers from family and friends. Everything looked beautiful.

In the basement, we set up pictures and Ryken's outfits for people to look at during the luncheon. The memory book was there as well. We set up a table with pictures of Grandma Isabelle, Granny, and Garret. It brought some comfort to know that Ryken was in heaven with them.

I looked at Granny's picture. She had ten children and had lost two of them. Her fourth child, Allan, had died from double pneumonia at the age of seven months. Allan had died four months after Granny's husband passed away unexpectedly. That was a double tragedy. Six years later, she gave birth to a stillborn daughter, her seventh child. Lillian Marie had passed away in the womb. I wish I could have talked to her. Her grief must have been heavy. I was so thankful that I still had Brett and Kaden in my life.

We left the church and drove to the funeral home. As I was getting out of my car, my mom's brother and his wife pulled up. I walked over to their vehicle and invited them to come inside to see Ryken. We would not be having an open casket, and it would be their last opportunity to see his beautiful face. They had not seen Ryken in person.

My aunt shook her head with sadness in her eyes and said, "I can't go in and see him."

I was not offended. I understood. I was so proud of him that I wanted to show him off. Even in death, I was still a proud mama.

My other cousins stood outside in support but would not come in to view the body. There is something very wrong about seeing a baby in a casket. Unfortunately, I was unable to introduce Ryken to them when he was alive since he was in the hospital for most of his life. Only a few family members and friends met him. He met so many nurses and doctors but hardly anyone we knew. I had to let it go.

As was custom, the family met in the basement of the church. Once the funeral began, we proceeded up the stairs and followed the casket down the aisle. The front pews were reserved for us. I held Brett's hand, and he carried Kaden in his other arm. Our family trailed behind us. As always, they supported us on this difficult day.

The service began, and the music we picked out was played. It was all a blur. I heard the sermon but was unable to take it in.

During the last week, as each of us considered the untimely death of baby Ryken, our hearts have been full of questions—chief amongst them being "how did this happen?" and "why did this happen?" These questions have not only been in the hearts and minds of Pam and Brett and their families but upon the lips of many of you here today—and indeed they have been heard throughout our community.

We are not here today to answer these questions—even if we could. Rather we are here to mourn—to mourn and to commend Ryken into God's care and to ask God to help us—and to most especially help Pam and Brett through this tragedy.

In the most beautiful of gardens, even those tended by the most skillful of botanists, there is an occasional rose that buds but never opens like all the others. Something keeps it from blooming. It fades away or disappears without having reached maturity.

What happens in nature's garden happens once in a while also in the garden of God's human family. A baby is born, beautiful, precious, but fails to come to its rightful unfolding. This child, like the bud that never fully opens, is gathered back into God's heavenly garden of souls. Where all imperfections are made perfect; all injustices made right; all mysteries are explained; and all sorrows turned to happiness.

Today we mourn our loss of such a child. We weep, just as Jesus himself wept at the death of his friend Lazarus. Even if we knew the answers to the questions that arise so naturally to our hearts and minds at times like this, there still would be no adequate explanation for this loss. It is painful.

And I believe it is also painful to God, who created the world intending for it to be perfect. As Jesus himself said in the reading that I shared earlier, "It is not the will of your Father that one of these little ones should perish."

And, as promised to us by God through the prophet Isaiah, there will come a time when there is a new heaven and a new earth, a time when never again will there be in it an infant who lives but a few days, or an old man who does not live out his years. A time so glorious in its presence that a person who dies at one hundred will be thought a mere youth and they who fail to reach one hundred will be considered accursed.

But this is not yet that time.

Rather this is the time when heaven yet remains above—and the earth below, a time when the joyful return of life is only experienced in its fullness once our mortal bodies perish. Much as a flower can come forth only after a seed or bulb is planted in the earth and loses its form.

There are angels above. Angels who watch over the little ones of this earth. Jesus speaks of them when he tells his disciples to be careful not to think less of little children simply because they are the children, for in heaven, he says, their angels continually see the face of my father in heaven.

There is a special place in the heart of God and amongst the angels for the little ones of this world. Just as there's a special place in our hearts today for Ryken.

And so we weep at what has happened. And so too, God weeps with us. What can be said that might ease the pain or assuage the grief that you and all of us feel today?

There isn't much we can say that will help. We can express our sympathy and sorrow. We can offer words of love, care and concern. We can say we will pray for you. But other than that, we don't know what to say about these things.

Maybe it is because people don't know what to say that they sometimes say the wrong things.

Some people may say that Ryken's death at this time was God's will. Don't believe them. The God we worship, the God who watches over us, doesn't will the death of babies or the pain of their parents. Many, many things that happen in this world are not the will of God. That is part of the price of the freedom we have been given by God.

Some people may say to you that God wanted Ryken in heaven with him. Well, I am confident God welcomed Ryken into his kingdom, I am sure God did not want him to die right now so that he could have him there.

Some people may seek to comfort you by saying to you that you are young and that you can have other children. That may be true, but other children will not replace Ryken. He was his own person. The empty place his death has left in your heart will not be filled simply because you have another child. Nor should it be. Every child is unique and precious.

I am sure the people who say things like this are saying them with the desire to comfort. They want to say something that will help. Bless them for it—but know that we are faced with a mystery—the mystery of life—and of death—in which there are no easy answers.

What, then, are we to say to these things?

What St. Paul's answer is, "If God is for us, who is against us? He who did not withhold his own Son, but gave him up for all of us, will he not with him also give us everything else?"

It is important to know that God is for you. God did not do this to you. God did not will Ryken's death or your pain. But God is with you in the midst of it all and will help you through it. God is for you. What is more, God gave up his own Son for us all.

Pam and Brett, God understands your pain. God has a Son who died also. Jesus died on the cross for us.

Now you may think, "Sure, but Jesus rose from the dead." Well, because Jesus rose to new life you can be confident that Ryken has new life also, one that can never be snatched away from him or from you. Today, in our grief, know your father said some days ago now, there's another angel in heaven. Cling to that hope, that promise of our God, and allow your tears to wash away the pain in the days and months to come.

Father finished his sermon, and continued with the Mass. I stared ahead, listening to every word but not retaining any. I realized there was a pause in the air.

Father was looking at me as I stared at the coffin. Ryken was not alone. He was resting with his stuffies and pictures of us with him inserted inside his casket. Ryken's picture—taken fourteen hours after he was born—was framed on the table beside the coffin. His teddy bear blanket from his crib was draped over the coffin, and the blue puppy was propped up on top. The blue puppy would watch over his little friend who was sleeping inside and would never awaken again. Ryken would never grow up to snuggle that blue puppy.

When it was my turn to speak, I walked up to the microphone and pulled courage from deep inside. My throat ached, and tears formed in my eyes. The tears landed on the paper I was trying to read. I was unable to stop them from coming.

All I could do was try to speak the words I had written. I latched on to the small ray of hope that all the people would hear these words from my heart through the tears that leaked out of the corners of my eyes and spilled down my face. I heard myself speak, but I was disconnected to my voice. It did not sound at all like me.

The average life span for an adult butterfly is twenty to forty days. Some species live no longer than three or four days. Others may live up to six months. Ryken is our butterfly.

Many of you may be thinking, "How can you go up there and give the eulogy?" Well, my thought is, "How could I not?" No one knows Ryken better than Brett and I. We are not going to be able to plan any Christmases, birthday parties, or other major life events for Ryken, so we took it upon ourselves to try our hardest to plan the most beautiful funeral we could for our son.

I'm here to tell you the life story of our beautiful baby boy: Ryken Addison Larocque.

In March, we found out we were pregnant. We decided to find out what we would be having. We decided we would not tell anyone that we knew.

At the ultrasound, the technician wrote on a piece of paper for us, "Congratulations, a little brother for Kaden." From that moment on, we had dreams of our boys growing up together, playing, fighting, doing what boys do.

During the months that followed, Brett and I could not agree on a name. The deal was that if Brett could not pick out a first and middle name, then my name would win. To make a long story short, Brett did not come up with a name I liked—and also he did not have a middle name picked out. Brett let me name him because of the pain I endured in labor. This made me very happy as I was calling the baby Ryken all along while I was pregnant. Ryken is German for "champion." Little did we know how significant his name would be. It was so fitting for Ryken because of everything he has been through.

As we patiently waited for the arrival of our baby, Brett got a new job in June so we were on the move to a different city on October 1. On October 18, my water broke, and we were off to the city we had just moved from to have our baby.

Ryken shot into this world at 7:44 p.m. Ryken was born so fast that he had a broken collarbone on his left side. He was an early birthday present as my birthday is on October 20. Ryken was 7 pounds and 10 ounces, and he was 21⅝ inches long. He had Brett's long legs, which I had predicted because of all the kicking he did inside of me.

Of course you feel a bond for the baby growing inside you, but now I understand the meaning of love at first sight. From the moment we laid eyes on Ryken, we were in love with him. The feeling of seeing your baby for the first time is indescribable. He had the most beautiful wavy, blond hair I have ever seen. He has every physical characteristic of Brett. His eyes, ears, nose, chin and body are an exact likeness of Brett.

Ryken did amazing the first eighteen hours of life. Ryken nursed right away and cluster fed that first night in the hospital. As he would drift off to sleep, I would lay him in his bassinet beside my bed. Ryken would wake up as soon as he was in there and cry. I would pick him up, and he would stop crying. After the fourth time of trying to get him to stay sleeping in his bassinet, I gave up. I picked him up, and he slept on my chest. There was a look on his face of such contentment at being held that I knew I was wrapped from that moment on.

The afternoon of October 19, I was changing his diaper, when Brett noticed Ryken had turned blue around his lips. He was admitted to neonatal intensive care unit. He spent nineteen days there, and there were many days that were up and down. Ryken had endured many blood tests, CAT scans, EEGs, and other medical procedures. Not many people got to meet Ryken outside of the medical world. The people he did meet will never forget him. Family, friends, doctors, and nurses all cared about our special baby boy.

We had a healer, Brita, come to the hospital and give him treatments. We had bought him a blue puppy that we named Brit after her. We truly believe it was because of Brita that Ryken got better and we were able to take him home on November 7.

We felt that everything was going to be okay as Ryken was nursing and eating more than what the doctors wanted. He had also been referred to as our "Miracle Baby" because of his strength and ability to do the opposite of what the doctors expected of him.

Ryken did not seem to mind his first bath at home, but he did not like any after that. When Ryken was hungry, he demanded to eat right away. He loved to be held and cuddled. He was an excellent traveler and always slept in the car. Anyone he met fell in love with him. We were thrilled to have him home.

We were worried about Kaden and how he would adapt to having a new baby around, after all his nickname is not King Kaden for nothing. Ryken was not so special at first, but when Kaden found out that the baby had bought him a Max doll from his favorite show, "Max and Ruby," having a baby brother was not so bad.

Once Ryken came home, Kaden fell in love with him also. He would come up to me and say, "Kiss baby," and gently kiss Ryken's head or cheek. Then he'd usually say, "Love him. Love baby Ryken." He did this numerous times each day.

Kaden would also peek into the bassinet and say, "Checking him" when asked what he was doing. Ryken opened his eyes a lot when Kaden would talk to him. They also developed their own special bond.

When I think of Ryken, I think of his sweet face, and how much he loved to cuddle. The most amazing thing in this world for both

Brett and I was to sit in our rocker recliner and put Ryken on our chests while he slept. No words could describe how this made us feel.

I prayed every day to God since October 19 and asked him to make Ryken better. I finally had to pray that God would take care of my baby and whatever plan he had for him would be. I am learning that in life, we do not have control over many things.

All of a sudden, Kaden ran up to me. He was crying and tugging on my leg. Brett was beside me and picked Kaden up. Kaden calmed down, and all three of us stood together as I finished Ryken's eulogy. Brett and Kaden stood with me, in support, as I said the hardest words of my life out loud to all the people at the funeral. Those kind people were showing their support and sympathy for our family. I gathered what was left of my courage and began speaking again.

On November 30, Ryken got sick again and had to go back into the hospital. I flew out with Ryken on the hospital plane to a children's hospital while Brett and his dad drove there through the night. Ryken was supposed to go to the pediatrics unit, but they had too many admissions that night so we were sent to the neonatal intensive care unit. Ryken had the most amazing neonatal Doctor, Dr. Uchi. He was so kind and caring about our son. We stayed in the parent room, which had a rocker recliner, a loveseat, and a queen-sized bed in it. We renamed it "Ryken's Room."

You can never explain the importance of minutes and hours when it comes to your last minutes and hours with your baby. We had to make the difficult decision to take Ryken off of life support on Saturday, December 3.

Ryken gave us eight days, sixteen hours, and thirty-three minutes to hold him, love him, cuddle him, and take about six hundred pictures. Luckily we had three different digital cameras.

The parent room is where we were with Ryken during his final days. At night, he would sleep between us. We told him that he did not have to be strong anymore and he could fly with the butterflies to heaven. The day before he passed away, he had his eyes open for over an hour and was looking at us. I knew that this was his gift and good-bye to us. Every night we had with him in that room was a blessing because we did not know if he would be with us the following day.

After Ryken had passed away, Kaden asked about him on the drive home. How do you explain to a two-and-a-half-year-old boy that his baby brother has gone to heaven?

I told him he was in heaven and was an angel now. Kaden started to cry and said, "No wings, Mommy. No wings, Mommy." I wonder if he understood me because he has not talked about Ryken to me since. During our last days with Ryken, we asked him to watch over Kaden and be his guardian angel.

Brett and I want to learn from Ryken's life. We want to remember that every single breath we breathe is monumental and sacred. We do not want to take anything for granted, and we want to cherish each day. That it is important to say how you feel, and it is important to ask for help. Friends are one of life's greatest gifts. Most importantly, how special our family is to us and our sons.

We want to remember that our parents and siblings were so caring and supportive during these eight weeks. That without them we would not be doing so good. Kaden was well cared for and given so much love when his mom and dad were away at the hospital all those days. Our family put their own lives on hold and rushed to be at our sides, visit with Ryken, and to take care of Kaden. It was difficult for them to lose a grandson and a nephew. We know it was hard to watch us go through this and not be able to take away the pain or bring us comfort. Just know that your presence during this time helped more than you'll know.

While getting pictures of Ryken done on Wednesday for his funeral, a lady shared that she had seven miscarriages and has no children. This really put things in perspective for us. To never have known Ryken, held Ryken, kissed Ryken, hugged Ryken, or loved Ryken is inconceivable. We are fortunate to have had the time we did.

Ryken, we love you and know that you flew with the butterflies to heaven and became an angel on Monday morning. Know that no matter how much time passes or what life has in store for us, we will never forget the precious weeks we spent together as a family. You are always in our thoughts and forever ingrained in our hearts. We love you, Ryken Addison, our champion. Rest in peace.

I felt the support of Brett and Kaden beside me as I finished reading. I was grateful that Kaden came up for me. We walked back to our pews. The end of the funeral was near. The motherly pride that came from sharing Ryken's life with everyone intertwined with the primal raw pain in my heart at knowing that soon he would be placed in the ground. I was trying my best to control my emotions. I wiped away tears and stuffed the anger and pain in the dark corners of my mind to contend with later.

I heard the priest speaking, and the funeral ended. Ryken's blue puppy was handed to me along with his folded blanket, revealing the beautiful coffin we picked out. Ryken was inside.

The music began, and we followed Ryken's coffin to the back of the church. Everyone's gaze was on us, and I tried to hold my head high. The pain in my chest was nearing an all-time high. I was barely holding on. I was unable to look at everyone staring at us. I found it hard to look at the little coffin with my baby inside.

The doors of the church opened. I felt the bitter cold on my face as my baby was loaded into the hearse. Brett, Kaden, and I got into the other car to drive to the graveyard. It was so bitterly cold—just like the temperature in my heart.

Numbness set in again, and I felt nothing inside but hollowness. I hugged Kaden to me and felt his warmth. "I love you, my sweet boy."

"Love you too," he said.

I told myself to breathe and keep it together. I was still trying to process the event, the day, the moment.

We pulled up to the open grave and watched them unload Ryken's coffin. They carried it over to the place he would be laid to rest. *What a dumb saying!* My baby's body would be in the ground soon and covered up with dirt. I had to leave him there in the freezing ground. *Laid to rest? Yeah right.*

I was holding Kaden's hand, and Brett was holding his other hand. It was only the three of us now.

"And baby makes four," my heart said.

"Not no more," my ego said.

We walked through the snow to Ryken's coffin. I stared at it and knew my baby was in there. *This is it. The final stage of leaving. I will never see his physical body again. I will never touch his hands or stroke his cheek.*

The anxiety traveled from my stomach to my heart. I was finding it hard to breathe. *Is it the cold or the anguish?* I tried to focus on the priest's words as he spoke about Ryken. I listened, but I was unable to take in what he was saying.

All I can see in my mind's eye is my baby in his coffin with his blue blanket with the airplane, butterfly, and car. I see him in Kaden's baptismal outfit and the stuffed animals surrounding him. He has his little giraffe, "Kass," beside him. All of it brings me little comfort. I feel guilty for keeping Ryken's blue puppy. I could not bear to part with it. I need the blue puppy to hold and snuggle when I miss Ryken. Forgive me, my baby.

Reality strikes again, and I realize he is alone. How can I leave him here all alone? I am glad Garret is just above him. In my mind, I tell Garret to watch out for him. *Take care of my baby. I will not be able to see him again. Ever.*

He will soon be in the ground. He will be covered with dirt. I am trying to stay in the confines of the reality of the moment. The mommy in me wants to lunge on top of the coffin and never let go. *It is not that big. I could carry it back with me to the car and leave. We would never have to be separated. No, you can't do that. You must remember Kaden and how he would react to seeing you come undone.* I feel like I am going crazy.

The priest speaks some more words. It is so cold, and I am worried about Kaden freezing. My good-bye to Ryken there is brief. I can barely function. Barely focus. Barely feel. I know that what is left of my heart has just crumbled into fine dust. Blown away, taken with the wind, never to be retrieved again—at least not right now.

I wonder how cold my baby is going to be in the cold ground. Left alone in the earth. All alone. I am thankful I put some stuffed animals and pictures of us in the coffin so his body is not alone. Garret is there above him. Thank God. Grandma is a few rows north, resting in peace.

A raging voice in my head screams at the world: *How am I to leave him here? I can't leave him here? You can't leave Ryken here? Don't leave him here!*

Ryken, Ryken, Ryken, I love you. I am so sorry to leave you. Mommy loves you, forever, and always. I am so sorry for leaving you here all alone. Forgive me. Forgive me. Forgive me.

The words swirl in my head, taking turns lunging at my composure. They try to make me break.

I feel myself disassociating from the moment. I feel myself slipping into a state of apathy.

"Good-bye, Ryken," I whisper.

I know he will not hear me and understand that I must go. I must leave him now—even though I do not know how.

I walk with Brett and Kaden to the car, and silence takes over my mind. For this, I am thankful.

CHAPTER 27

A Luncheon We Will Go

I t was as though something has entered my body and was helping direct me. It was called shock, sent to me to deal with my pain, and I welcomed it with open arms. I was on autopilot. It was no different than a traffic cop directing traffic. Stop. Go. Wait. Proceed.

It was as though I was in a robotic state as we rode back to the church for the luncheon. Kaden's words went in one ear and trickled out the other side. I nodded. His words were colliding with the thoughts circulating in and out of my brain.

Many thoughts were running through my mind. I didn't want to face everyone and listen to the voices that would repeat, "I am so sorry for your loss." I didn't want to see their pity or pain and know that their lives were so good while mine was upside down.

Though the words that they would say were appreciated, they changed nothing. Ryken was gone, and God did not answer my miracle. Nothing would make it better. Nothing. No words. No one could help me. God did nothing to help me either. Ryken was dead.

We went into the church for the lunch that was customary to provide for the funeral. It was the last thing I wanted to do. I had no appetite and no desire to sit through lunch talking to people. I felt sorry for those who were lining up to share their condolences. What can a person say? *Sorry for your luck, my friend.* No offense to anyone, but I didn't want to hear any of it. Instead, I offered a smile and thanked them for coming.

Brett did not have much to say either. I heard some of the words being said to us and heard the compliments. *That was a beautiful eulogy.* My ears perked up; those words did bring me comfort. I wanted it to be perfect for Ryken. We thanked everyone. It was another memory for the old memory box. To hear that it was "a very touching and beautiful service" helped me somewhat. It was another reminder that Ryken was here. I might be able to be grateful someday that all of these people cared about Ryken, about us, and about our family enough to show up for the service. They were celebrating in some fashion that Ryken was real—that he was born and lived. It was a short life, but he existed.

I heard Kaden giggling. He was laughing and smiling with the grandparents. Kaden was a great distraction for my grief. It looked like the grandparents were using him for their own grief as well.

Many people wanted to speak with us. Most of them had been at our wedding. None of us would have guessed they would be at our baby's funeral three and a half years later, lining up with their sympathies.

I stood with my close friends who had babies around the time Ryken was born. They each gave me a hug. None had their babies with them. I briefly thought it was thoughtful of them. I was so happy their babies were healthy. I was not jealous or envious of their luck. I was not upset that they had living babies while I did not. I truly cared about each of these ladies and their families. I would not wish what we had just been through on anyone. I viewed their babies as a way for me to watch Ryken grow if he had lived. I thanked them for coming and saw the helplessness in their eyes as they left quietly.

When lunch was over, we cleaned up. My baby's funeral had gone off without a hitch. I was happy with the outcome. Once everything was over, I felt the emotional exhaustion from the day.

We asked our siblings, Ryken's godparents, to meet us upstairs for a picture with Ryken's framed picture. We walked up to the main area of the church. I tried hard not to remember that Ryken had been there in his coffin a few hours ago—and now was in the ground all alone.

I forced myself back to the present moment and looked through my camera. They lit Ryken's baptismal candle. *A picture is worth a thousand words.* No matter how many candles were lit, the reality was that Ryken's light had been snuffed out. We gathered up his belongings, his picture, the candles, and the flowers. These things were what remained of my baby, proving he was indeed here.

The rational side of my brain kicked in. I was grateful for the pictures of Ryken's godparents. It was another piece that would be added to the memories of Ryken's life. *He was here. See? These were his godparents. They lit a candle for him. He was alive and real and my beautiful baby boy. Ryken Addison.*

We headed back to my parents' farm with my family. I was unable to think beyond that day. We had friends who were getting married the next night, but there was no way I could go to the wedding. I sent them a silent prayer of congratulations.

Brett, Kaden, and I slept well that night and headed home the next day. A room was still prepared for a baby who was no longer there. God had decided that baby needed to live in heaven instead of in our house. I would see Ryken's bassinet, but I would not see Ryken.

The reality of my loss was settling in. Like a heavy fog on a cold winter day, it was difficult to see through it.

CHAPTER 28

Life Goes On—or Does It?

O nce the funeral was over, I continued on autopilot. I had been sleeping well, which was a saving grace in itself. I was quite tired, but I believed my body was trying to adjust to everything. My hormones were trying to balance out since I was no longer nursing or pumping. My beautiful Kaden was my reason for putting two feet on the floor each morning and hauling my grief-stricken body out of bed.

I looked at the calendar six days before Santa would arrive. Oh my goodness. Like every year at this time of year, Christmas music was playing everywhere. The song that hurt my heart was "Where Are You Christmas?" by Faith Hill. *Where are you Ryken?* It made me want to scream and cry. I changed the radio station and suppressed my anger.

My mom and I went shopping to bring Christmas home to Kaden. He was only two and a half, and it was not fair to wallow in pain and have him miss Christmas because of my grief. Thank goodness Santa and his elves had been on task all year.

I decided to go into a craft store in search of Ryken's Christmas stocking. I never go to Michael's, but I needed a stocking to put under the tree for him. Christmas music was playing, people were rushing around, and frenzied energy was in the air. I was barely surviving. There were random moments where I couldn't really breathe. I said a prayer that Faith Hill's song would not come on in the store.

I found the most beautiful little red and white stocking with a capital "R" stitched in red.

This is it! That was so easy. I love this little stocking.

I headed toward the checkout line to pay.

This is going well. So far, so good.

My anxiety had been under control. I just had to get Kaden's gifts before I went home. Skates and a hockey helmet for my sunshine were next on my to-do list. I was almost home free.

This is not so bad. I am doing okay. I can do this.

I was at the front of the store, and a woman rushed over. I tried to avoid eye contact, but she was smiling. "Hi Pam. How is Ryken doing?"

I felt a blow to my stomach.

Has someone punched me? No, I still hear the Christmas music.

I tried to catch my breath. I was still at Michael's. I needed to answer her question. I could barely form any words. My eyes welled up, and tears began to fall.

It was one of the moms I had met in neonatal. She and her baby were lucky. They were discharged and left NICU before us. She appeared to be doing fine. She should be. Her baby was alive. She would celebrate Christmas with her baby.

I looked at her and said, "He died on December 12."

Her face registered pure shock. She stepped toward me and touched my arm. "I am so sorry."

Tears filled my eyes, and it was hard to see clearly. I tried desperately not to lose it. I just wanted to buy Ryken's Christmas stocking and go home. I held it tightly and tried to breathe through my pain. The pain in my stomach navigated toward my chest and lodged in my throat. It was blocking my speech. I had no other words for her. "Thank you."

Just leave me alone now—and don't ask me any more questions.

I knew she felt my pain. Maybe my face said it all.

We had shared a common bond of being neonatal postwar veterans, but that was where it ended. She had won her battle. I had lost mine. She would always be the victor. Every smile, every milestone, and every birthday she shared with her living baby was what I would miss out on with mine. She was on the high road home to joy. My journey down the path of grief and despair had just begun. I was heading toward the pits of hell. There was no detour or any way of avoiding it. I was going to crash and burn. Merry, merry Christmas.

I paid for the stocking and decided to get the rest of the gifts another day. I said a silent prayer that I was grateful we had moved to a different city where no one knew us. I could go shopping, and no one would recognize me. I would be anonymous. Just another face in the crowd.

Even the task of getting groceries would be easier without someone asking where my baby was. I would not have to say those words again for a while. No one would even know I had been pregnant. No one would ask about Ryken. I would not have to say those words again. Knowing it was hard enough. Saying it out loud almost killed me.

I still had a Christmas to plan for my toddler. My beautiful, energetic Kaden was waiting for me at home. I had new demons that I was fighting off daily. I was beginning to carry the demons on my back. I named them guilt and worry. I was fixated on how the loss of Ryken affected Kaden. The social worker inside me kicked in and asked how my grief was affecting his development? My poor Kaden.

I asked myself how scarred was he from the past eight weeks: being separated from us, seeing his mom and dad periodically, and meeting his new baby brother one day and being told he was gone the next. Kaden had no concept of time. It was like Ryken was there, and then he was gone. I told him his brother went to heaven. What thoughts were running through his head? Gone where? What is heaven? I remember his words *no wings*.

As an adult, it was hard to understand where Ryken was. How was my toddler going to comprehend or begin to formulate an understanding of it? I could barely do it.

Maybe Kaden knows more than I do.

CHAPTER 29

Many Signs to Ease My Pain

A few days before Christmas, I was going through the mail. There was a receipt for Ryken's funeral. The funeral home had exceeded any expectations we had. Everything had gone as planned and as we had hoped for.

Brett took out the trash the next morning. It was cold, and I was thankful he was doing it instead of me. We did not have gender-specific tasks in our home, but I didn't love taking out the garbage in the winter.

A few minutes later, he came back inside and said, "I saw the neighbor. He asked how the baby was doing and what we had."

I realized our new neighbors didn't know about Ryken yet. We had met them briefly when we moved in a couple of weeks before Ryken's birth. They had a daughter a few months younger than Kaden and were a really nice family.

"What did you tell him?" I asked.

"I said we had a baby boy and that he had died."

"What did John say to that?" I asked.

"I think I shocked him." Brett said his reply was, 'I'm sorry to hear that'.

It sounded like an uncomfortable conversation. I guess you never know what you may hear when you are taking out the trash.

"Well, what did you say to him?"

"I said thanks, and I came in the house."

"That's it?"

Brett looked at me and said, "Yeah."

Okay. I guess they know now. I actually felt bad for John. He'd probably never ask another expectant couple about their baby unless he saw a living baby with them. That was the ripple effect of how losing a baby affected those around you.

I returned to my stack of mail. There was another letter from my good friend's mother. She shared how her own mother had lost a child when he was an infant. It was never talked about in the home, but it was a source of great sadness to the mother. It was many years ago, but the pain she endured was no different than mine. She had a treasure box with her baby's special items in it: clothes, shoes, and his baby spoon.

It was so thoughtful of my friend's mom to take the time to handwrite a letter to me. I felt like I was not alone in my loss. I knew I was one of many out there. Brett's own grandmother had lost two children as infants. There were others within our extended family. There were grieving mothers and dads everywhere. It was just not talked about. It was almost a taboo subject.

There was a package addressed to all three of us, and I didn't recognize the name on the return address. My curiosity was piqued as I opened the typed letter.

Dear Pam, Brett, and Kaden,

We, my sister and I, along with our families, would like to extend our sincerest sympathy to you and all of your family. We realize that you probably don't even know who we are. That doesn't matter. We are family. Our clan is a pretty special bunch, and we are very proud to be a part of that. We have learned from them that in times of happiness and in times of trial we must stand together. Our generation must continue. So we offer our hearts to you at this tragic time in your young lives. We belong to your Aunt Lynn's family. Our mom is Martha. Know that you are in our thoughts and prayers. Not just this day. We hope this angel will be a reminder to you that people like us that you don't even really know, are praying for you and thinking about you. The bear is a little something for Kaden. We are very saddened that life has handed you this tragic loss. Take care of yourselves.

Sincerely,

The names were listed but they meant nothing to me. I was unable to place faces with the names. The words touched me so profoundly. I wiped my tears as I read the letter. I touched the soft white bear with the angel wings. The special gift for Kaden was so kind.

I was deeply moved by the letter. The kindness, prayers, and thoughts really moved me. It was days after the funeral and it was as if Ryken was not even there for the rest of the world. Everyone else's life went on. I was left asking, "Where are you, Ryken?"

I called my dad and shared the letter and the names with him. He was able to explain who they were, and I recognized my great-aunt and her daughter. They were the daughters and granddaughters of the ladies I knew. There would be a birthday celebration in the spring, and the ladies would be there. I told my dad I planned to attend so I could thank them personally for their thoughtful gift and kind words.

I looked through the pile of mail. There was a letter from my cousin. Seraphina and I were kindred spirits and had a lot in common. I opened the letter, which was written on December 17, the day after Ryken's funeral.

Dear Pam,

I have done an angel card reading for you, and this is the card I received. It is from Angel Sonya. She brings you a message from your deceased loved one: "I am happy, at peace, and I love you very much. Please don't worry about me." The additional message is this as well: "Your heart has been heavy with grief, and I'm here to reassure you. I am a guardian angel to your deceased loved one, and I want you to know that there is no reason for you to worry. Your loved one is very happy and has adjusted to the transition very well. There is no anger or upset directed toward you, only love and understanding. You have done nothing wrong, dear one, so please don't blame yourself in any way. You did everything that you could, and your loved one has asked me to share this appreciation with you. You and your loved one still share great love between your souls. That love could never die, although you miss your loved one's physical presence, you have already connected spiritually in your dreams as well as through feeling, hearing, smelling, or seeing your loved one's essence. Your loved one is as alive as you are—even more alive in many ways. Relieved of earthly cares or bodily pain, your loved one is freer and happier than ever. As soon as you complete your life's purpose and it is your time to make the transition, you will be reunited in each other's arms. In the meantime, please know

that your loved one is with you often and
that the angels surround you continuously."

The cards she had used were Doreen Virtue's "Messages
From Heaven." She had begun doing angel card readings a
few months earlier. Her letter brought me some comfort as
well. Her thoughtfulness did not go unnoticed.

Seraphina was sending me love, and I was in her
prayers. She gave me a small figurine that fit in the palm
of my hand. It was a toddler with wings, sleeping with
his teddy bear on a pillow. I placed it on my nightstand
beside my lamp. I could tell it would bring me comfort every
morning and night.

Mindy gave me a small pillow that I keep on my
nightstand. I keep my favorite picture of Ryken in it. It was
taken just before he turned a month old. Every night, I say
good night to Ryken before I shut off my lamp. The blue
puppy sleeps beside me as well. Kaden has not claimed
it yet; for now, I keep it safe. It gives me great comfort to
keep those things with me. The visual reminders help me
to remember that Ryken was real and not a dream. I was
unable to move them, and God help me if they were ever
lost. It was almost like a ritualistic tribute to him that
helped me grieve and find some sense of peace each day.

I also wore the butterfly necklace that my mom gave me
when Ryken was in the children's hospital. I felt like Ryken
was with me when I wore the necklace. I only took it off at
night when I got ready for bed. My grief was welling over
and overflowing. The little daily rituals gave me a sense of
control in a world I had no control over. As a human and a
grieving mother, I tried to keep a tight rein over what was
within my control. Honestly, it wasn't much.

On Christmas Eve, a visitor came to our house. Adam,
the astrologist, stopped by for a visit on his way home for
the holidays. Although it was difficult to visit right then, I
made a concession. Adam had been very kind during our
time in Ryken's Room. He had given me the information that

Ryken's life purpose was to be a teacher. That information brought me some comfort as well.

I told Adam I planned to contact a psychic or a medium to see if I could talk to Ryken. I had told him about a man my sisters had seen and liked. Adam had a friend who was a medium and a psychic. Jenny lived in a nearby city and did crossovers. He had her phone number and would call me once he returned home. I was overcome with excitement. I needed to speak to Ryken. I needed to know he was okay.

If I had not been sick with the iron poisoning, I would not have met Adam. He was a close friend of the healer who had helped me then.

Life is never what you think it will be. Though you don't understand the why at the time, it's important to trust. That is not always easy, especially as a grieving mother. Especially when you were handcuffed to your ego. Especially when the key was missing to the handcuffs. Especially when you sat with your ego most of the time. Only when I was sleeping was I completely free of my ego.

I was more at peace after Adam's visit. I knew I would talk to Ryken soon. The news lifted a thin layer of grief off of my heart. I finally had some optimism and hope.

We began our Christmas tradition by giving Kaden one gift on Christmas Eve. He opened it up, and it was new pajamas. They were light blue with cars on them. It was his first two-piece set and had a button-up top. He loved them. He looked so big in them, and there was a sense of normalcy taking place again for me. I was again working hard at staying focused in the present moment and searching deep within for some Christmas Eve cheer. Truthfully, knowing I would be talking to Ryken soon made the cheer within easier to find.

Kaden was ready for bed. The next day would be Christmas—our first of many without Ryken. I would never have guessed three months earlier when I was pregnant that my Christmas would be without our baby. While we were settling in and painting our new home, not once did it cross my mind that Ryken would not be there for Christmas. After the Trisomy 18 scare, I never worried about anything regarding my baby or his health.

It was my new reality to live a life without our baby. I tried to stay in the moment and snuggle with Kaden. He said good night to his grandparents. Brett and I tucked him in and read a Christmas bedtime story. Within minutes of finishing it, Kaden was asleep. We told him if he was awake when Santa came, then Santa wouldn't stop at our house.

I gazed down at him and said another silent prayer of deep gratitude for him. He would bring me Christmas spirit in the morning. He was a true blessing. I said a silent prayer that he was born without NKH. *Thank you, God, for this favor.*

My parents stayed with us overnight on Christmas Eve. On Christmas morning, I was occupied with opening gifts and visiting with family. For Kaden, always for my sunshine, I would try my best.

By the Christmas tree, we had Ryken's framed picture from his funeral with his stocking hanging on the top corner. I looked at it and felt some peace. Having his picture and little stocking as part of the celebration included him in a physical way. If we had done nothing, I would have felt like he was forgotten already. I needed to see his picture, and I needed a stocking for him.

Kaden made our Christmas wonderful. Santa brought him his first pair of skates, along with a helmet to protect his head. After burying my baby who had a brain that was completely damaged, I was even more anal about Kaden's safety and his brain. We had control over him wearing a helmet. Why would I not take every precaution to ensure Kaden's head was always protected no matter what he was doing?

I felt a deeper sense of awareness and protectiveness toward Kaden—if that was even possible. I was already quite the helicopter parent before everything happened.

He could be all we would ever have. He was priceless. That was what his middle name meant. I did not know how true that would turn out to be when we named him. I sure knew it now.

The other gifts were opened, and Kaden was having so much fun. His joy was contagious, but there was still heaviness in my heart. I made myself smile and tried to stay in the moment.

My mom gave me a charm bracelet. I could have pictures made into charms to personalize the bracelet. I chose my favorite pictures of Kaden and Ryken and used them for the charms. That was my favorite Christmas present.

We wished Brett's mom a merry Christmas over the phone. We had plans to visit the following day. She told us that an aunt of Brett's wanted a picture of Ryken to make a round Christmas tree ornament. I just had to pick out a picture. That was another wonderful gift. I would decide on a picture with Brett's help.

Christmas rolled out as quietly as it came in. I was relieved when it was over. It was painful... and I was numb. When I thought about Kaden, I felt guilty about those thoughts. He was such a sweet boy, and I was thankful we had all of our family to help us with him. We needed all the support we could get.

CHAPTER 30

Talking to Ryken

I called Jenny on December 27. I had made myself wait through Christmas and Boxing Day, which was very difficult. I was learning patience slowly. I was able to set up an appointment for December 31. Only four days away—I could feel joy in my heart again. The next few days would be hard since my excitement was growing stronger every day. As each minute passed, I was closer to speaking to my baby. I was feeling renewed.

I am coming, Ryken. We will talk soon, my sweet boy!

On December 29, Deann and her husband visited. We decided to go to the outdoor rink to have Kaden try out his new skates. Skates were tied, and we were ready. Helmet was securely in place. The air was crisp, and I could see my breath.

When Kaden stepped onto the ice for the first time, he took a few steps and fell down. He did not look very happy. We encouraged him to get up and try again.

Deann was skating by and calling out to him to catch her.

Kaden stood up and tried to take another step, but he fell down again. He looked at his aunty skating with ease and shouted, "I want Aunty Dea's skates! Mine are broken!"

I was laughing hard because he was so serious. "Kaden, you have to learn how to skate. Your skates are not broken."

He got up and tried again. After a few more steps, he fell again. He began to cry and said, "See? They are broken! I already know how to skate. I want Aunty Dea's skates."

We decided that the skating lesson was over for the day. Timbit hockey might not be on the horizon, but it sure felt good to laugh. I felt a bit guilty for doing so.

The day finally arrived, bringing a lot of snow and wind. It was New Year's Eve, but we had no plans for celebrating that night. It would be a quiet night at home with Kaden. I gathered my purse and kissed Kaden and Brett good-bye. I hugged them and smiled as I closed the door. I drove into the big city for my two thirty meeting. I had to reschedule due to the poor weather.

Typically I would not go out in that kind of weather, but these were different circumstances. I was going to talk to the dead. I hated the word "dead." I knew Ryken would come. I was just hoping he was okay.

It was stormy during the beginning of the drive. Snow was falling, and the wind was blowing it all over the place. I would typically be anxious and stressed out. I had a different feeling inside. A calmness and knowingness circulated through my body. I knew with all my heart that I was going to be okay. I would arrive at my appointment safely. All I could do was sing to the radio and smile to myself. I did not care because I needed to see Jenny. I needed her to help me connect with Ryken.

I parked and walked into a little shop on a one-way street. The warmth of the store hit me in the face as I opened the door. There were crystals everywhere, and other unique objects were for sale. I was not there to shop though.

I walked directly to the counter and said, "Hi, my name is Pam. I am here for my reading with Jenny."

Within minutes, I met the most wonderful woman. She had beautiful sparkling eyes and the warmest smile. Being in her presence was like having the rays of the sun beaming down on you on the warmest day in July. She introduced

Ryken's Journey

herself and welcomed me into a little room. She closed the door behind us and offered me some tea.

Once we were seated, she asked what had I come to see her for. I began to speak about Ryken. Unlike many in society, I was not skeptical at all. I shared that I really wanted to talk to my baby.

Jenny was very frank with me. The youngest person she had talked to was a five-year-old boy. She was very clear that she did not know what would happen. She was unsure if his spirit would come—and even if she could talk to a baby. Her next words were music to my ears. She said, "We'll try and see what happens."

I had enough hope for both of us. I knew beyond a shadow of a doubt that Ryken would come in the next few minutes. I would get to talk to him, and I would know he was okay. I was praying he was okay. I was so giddy inside with excitement and anticipation that I could hardly sit still.

We sat down: lights off, candles lit, and tea prepared. When everything was in order, Jenny explained that she needed to validate that it was Ryken for both of us. She explained how there's our side here on earth and the other side where Ryken was.

She closed her eyes and began moving her fingertips on the desktop. She began speaking. She was relaying to me that she saw a two- or three-year-old boy with an angel. The angel's name was Sonya.

When she asked why Ryken came to her at that age, he said, "Babies don't talk."

Wow, that is the truth. I was struck speechless for a moment, but then I laughed. He was so funny and cheeky. In my mind, I could see Ryken talking to me. He was Kaden's age. I pictured Ryken as blond with Brett's skin coloring.

I could easily relate to Ryken that way. It would be like chatting with Kaden. I was in awe that he was smart enough to come at that age with his angel.

225

Sonya was another gift for me. I had received the letter from Seraphina ten days earlier. That letter notified me that Ryken was with Angel Sonya and was doing well. He had transitioned and was free of any bodily pains. Angel Sonya's message was that I was to release my grief and know that my baby was still with me. He was happy, and we were still connected. We would always share a great love for each other. I was talking with him and the angel that was caring for him. Talk about validation. I was speechless.

Jenny closed her eyes and said, "He is wearing a white T-shirt and a diaper. I am asking him for something to validate to you that it is truly him. Again it has to be something that will convince me as well." Jenny listened with her eyes closed. "He wants me to tell you the word *giraffe*. He said you would know what it means."

I could feel a smile of joy radiating out of my mouth and tugging my lips upward. Of course this was my beautiful baby Ryken!

I told Jenny that Ryken was referring to the giraffe from the children's hospital. I explained how his night nurse had bought the giraffe for him because his Mohawk hair reminded her of Ryken's blonde hair that also resembled a Mohawk. Jenny seemed okay that it was validation enough for both of us. I knew it was my baby. *Ryken came to talk to me just like I knew he would.*

Ryken wanted me to know that his legs did not hurt anymore. He was referring to the muscle biopsy during the genetic testing. I had been carrying guilt about that. He told Jenny that the biopsies did not hurt him, and I was relieved beyond measure.

Ryken wanted her to tell me that his feet were not cold anymore because he was wearing his slippers. We had buried Ryken in the brown slippers I had bought for him when I was pregnant. The funny coincidence was that we had been gifted an identical pair that I had in his room at home. It was nice to hear that he liked his slippers and that his feet were warm.

With a laugh, Jenny said, "He is quite the chatterbox. The angel that is with him is nodding." Jenny kept her eyes closed as she listened. "I can see she has a tight grip on his hand. Ryken is very excited and energetic right now. Angel Sonya had to bring him to us for this visit. Over there, he is still young—and he does not understand everything that happened during his time on earth."

I was writing down notes and reeling with the fact that Ryken was in the arms of an angel. My entire body was buzzing with energy.

Jenny said, "Ryken will go to something similar to school over there. He will decompress and learn about his time on earth. That is where his soul will learn about what he has been through during this lifetime."

I said, "What lessons did Ryken want me or others to learn?"

The next words relayed to me gave me shivers. I call them "angel hug" shivers because my whole body trembled like I was cold—even though the room was warm.

Jenny said, "It was about the lessons Ryken chose to learn. He only wanted to learn about the birth and dying processes. He did not want to live to be sixty or seventy years old."

Just like that, he answered the question that had been banging around in my head like a Ping-Pong ball.

"Why did I lose my baby?"

We signed up to help him by being his parents. The fact that I signed up to lose my baby and watch him die shed some light on my grief. He had to have a rare genetic condition in order to complete his life lessons in a short amount of time. That explained why he had such a difficult birth, life and death. My question had been answered for the moment.

Jenny said, "He also wanted to learn about relationships while he was here."

I was a bit dumbfounded. My family was *very* unique. Ryken's palliative care days were so difficult and emotional for all the family members who were involved. Each person supported us during our darkest hours. That time together brought us closer, and each of us took something away from the life-changing experience we shared with Ryken. He taught all of us something.

"Did he ever pick a good family to be born into!"

He knew what kind of family and relationships he would get when he chose us. I guess we all signed up to help him and learn for ourselves as well. Those words were really helping me process my grief in a different way than I had expected.

I was beginning to shift my mind-set. I pushed my ego aside for the moment and listened to my higher self.

Jenny said, "This is about Ryken's life. This time in your life was for Ryken to learn about the birth process. Living as a human baby who will eventually die. It was for Ryken's soul to grow so he could experience what it is like to die." I began to realize that I had been focusing on my human ego's need to have and want two boys to raise.

My higher self said, "You and Brett signed up to be the loving parents that Ryken needed in order to fulfill his life's purpose. All of your family knew on a soul level what the outcome would be. Everyone is interconnected. Your souls knew what the outcome would be. Pam, your ego and heart are working together against the soul's lessons. That is your grief—and that is what a human goes through when processing the death of a loved one, especially a child, a baby. Now is the time to align your heart with your soul as you gently show your ego the door, while you kindly and respectfully ask it to leave."

I was in awe, and my soul knew that Ryken was safe. My heart knew it too. My heart was full of love, and I felt a sense of peace. For the moment, everything was all right in my world. I had a deep gratitude that Angel Sonya was watching my precious Ryken.

Jenny's words made everything better. "Ryken was talking about the teddy bear mobile over his crib at home.

He was talking about you playing with it in his room. He was with you when you did that." Just hearing the words was healing. Knowing that Ryken had been in his room since his passing made me happy. He was with me when I played his mobile and watched his teddy bears dance in a circle as my tears fell like rain. I had watched the mobile and been so full of grief that there was no baby in the crib to hug and love.

Ryken had been there with me energetically, but I could not feel him through my pain. I had to try to move through my pain to feel him there with me. I had some work to do.

"Ryken has been in your house since he has been on the other side. He was telling me that he goes 'brrr' from the draft by the front door."

I began to laugh. I was full of joy that his spirit was with us at home. I sat in the chair many times crying with empty arms. My heart was aching to hold Ryken again. I was unable to understand why Ryken was gone. Why did God take him away from me?

So many thoughts raced through my head. "Will Ryken come back and reincarnate with another baby in our family?" I didn't realize it, but I was holding my breath while I waited for a response.

Jenny began talking about Brett and asking questions about him. She said, "Does your husband have some kind of eye twitch or nervous tic?"

I replied, "No."

"Is there a habit Brett does when he gets stressed out?"

"Yes. He chews his nails."

Jenny said, "Ryken just told me he does not like that—and Dad would have to quit that habit if he comes back."

"Okay." I smiled. *I'll tell your dad, my beautiful boy!*

Jenny said, "Ryken was talking about a puppy."

"Oh? I know he was talking about the blue puppy we gave him in the hospital."

She shook her head. "No. He was talking about a real puppy. He was telling me that if he comes back here—and he was very clear about this—that he wants you to get him a real puppy."

I looked at Jenny, and I really didn't know what to say. *Okay,* I thought, *Kaden would love a puppy.*

I, however, did not want a puppy. I wanted a real baby to hold and care for—not a puppy. I was a little taken aback by all the information I was receiving. I felt my head nodding. "Does Ryken know if we are going to have more children?"

She was listening to him, eyes closed. She looked directly at me and said, "He wants to know what you think about a baby girl?"

My heart leaped with hope. I was so excited. We had still not received the genetic testing. We didn't even know if we could have another child at all. *A girl is coming for us?* Joy was exploding in my body like fireworks at a celebration. "I would love a baby girl!"

Jenny asked, "Ryken wants to know if you would put ribbons in his hair?"

I was grinning from ear to ear. "I don't have to if he does not want me to." I said through my smile.

Jenny said, "Ryken said you could. He wouldn't mind that." She recommended waiting eight months before trying to have another baby. Ryken would be "decompressing" and "learning", over the next few months, about what he went through on earth. He would not be reincarnating before that.

Ryken told Jenny to tell me that August would be a good time to start trying to have another baby. Ryken would decide later if he was coming back or not. He would be the one to make the choice about whether he came back or not during this lifetime.

I guess it's not up to me. I was slowly learning that I had very little control in this life.

Jenny told me that Angel Sonya smiled and said it was a possibility that Ryken's soul would reincarnate with the next baby. She reiterated to me that Angel Sonya was very protective of Ryken.

Hearing those words made me so happy. My question had been answered. I was at peace for now.

Jenny told me that Ryken was concerned about my mom. "Ryken said Grandma has changed since his death. 'If she does not let go of her anger, she will be going before her time.'"

I was not ready to lose her yet. She had taken Ryken's death very hard and cried whenever his name was mentioned. I knew it hurt her tremendously to watch us going through our loss. The feeling of helplessness can be difficult for a parent. I know it firsthand from my experience with Ryken.

Jenny said, "He said for you to tell Dad the word *Toby*. He will know what Ryken is talking about."

I did not know the name, but I would share it with Brett. I was curious about who Toby was and what Brett would say or think about it.

Jenny said, "Ryken was telling me about a charm bracelet and he really likes that idea."

I told her about my charm bracelet. One of the pieces of the charm bracelet had a picture of Ryken on it. It was validation that Ryken was with us for Christmas. He was still with me except in a different way. Ryken knew what was going on in our lives and was right there beside us. We just could not see him, but his spirit was there. I had to work on feeling him with me at home.

I was curious about what he looked like on the other side. I asked if Ryken's hair was blond.

Jenny confirmed he had blond hair, but there was auburn in it as well. He was getting freckles across the bridge of his nose and on his cheeks.

This physical description was beyond wonderful. My heart sang with joy. It was as if I was blind but could see now.

Jenny said, "Would you like to feel your son?"

"Yes!" I said with wonder in my trembling voice.

Jenny closed her eyes again and listened to what Ryken was telling her. Than she grabbed a piece of paper and began to write. When she finished writing, she turned it over so I could not read it.

I closed my eyes, calmed my breathing by taking some deep breaths to ground myself, and waited. Within a few seconds, I could feel pressure on my chest and coolness around my face. I breathed as I felt many emotions, but the strongest one was love. It lasted for a few moments, and I truly felt serene. I felt the urge to open my eyes.

I took a deep breath and shared with Jenny what I had just felt and experienced. I explained how my chest and heart felt warm, yet there was a coolness around my face. I had no idea what was written on the paper or what Ryken's plans for me were.

She turned over the paper and pushed it across the table for me to read it. "Should feel him around knees and lap, possibly feel breathing on face as he whispers, 'Mommy.'"

I began to softly cry as if a piece of heaven had just touched me.

Jenny said, "Ryken is still in your lap."

I smiled, closed my eyes, and took another deep breath. I felt the warmth and pressure around my chest and the coolness near my face return. I hugged myself, feeling Ryken in my arms. "I love you, Ryken." I was holding the essence of heaven within my arms. The warmth surrounding me had a calming, euphoric effect on me. I basked in the moment and felt the connection with my baby again. The aching pain in my chest disappeared, and I could feel pure, unconditional love from Ryken. His love and gratitude were the gift he gave me because I had given him the greatest gift of all. I had chose to be his mother in this lifetime.

My eyes were still closed. I did not want to break the connection with him.

Jenny said, "He has his hands on either side of your face. Ryken has great love for you. He just said, "I love you, Mommy."

Tears formed in my eyes. I couldn't hold them back any longer. My body was vibrating with the energy that Ryken was sending to my heart. It was as though he was trying to heal it with a vibrational touch from the other side. Feeling and knowing Ryken was connecting to my heart, touching my face with his little hands and saying, "I love you Mommy", cured any skepticism that had ever tried to play with my ego.

I was shuddering from the inside out. There was no doubt in my mind that Ryken and I would have a soul-to-soul connection forever. It would always transcend time and space, and that moment proved it.

I was overwhelmed with emotions. The tears were rushing forth, and I allowed them to fall as the floodgates opened. I released the pain and anguish I had been holding in for so long. It was pure love—unconditional love for my beautiful baby. I missed him so much, and living without him was unbearable. I knew, on a deeper level, that I would live. I had to.

Luckily, I was still sane enough to know that I had to continue to live for Kaden's sake. I was admitting the truth to myself. *Living at this present moment is very painful for me. That is why I came here.* As a mother whose baby had just passed away, I needed answers. That meeting was imperative for my own mental health. It was about me—and my own life lessons.

As the tears subsided, I was back in a state of pure wonder and awe. It was an amazing experience for me, and I was in awe of Jenny and her gift. I felt new emotions envelop me, and I made room in my body for something other than pain. There was a peacefulness I had not felt for a long time. I had a sense of happiness after feeling Ryken in my lap and hugging him close to my broken heart.

Jenny's voice continued in my ear like the most beautiful song I had ever heard. "Angel Sonya helped Ryken jump into your lap. She waited beside you until he was finished. Then she grabbed his hand when he jumped back down. She is very protective of him." I was relieved to know how loved and cared for my baby was on the other side.

The pressure in my chest was gone, but I still felt the peace in my body. My heart was not hurting as much. Some healing within must have occurred.

Jenny said, "Ryken is still around because of the pain you are feeling. He wants you to know that he never meant to hurt you and that he loves you very much." Her eyes were closed as she listened to the words Ryken and the angel shared with her.

I knew the words she was speaking were true, but I was sad because Ryken was not there for me to raise. He was my second son, and I wanted him with me so badly. I believed he would be all right. I had lived on hope for so long that it was hard to make my heart understand that it no longer existed in the way I had dreamed and prayed it would.

I needed to discuss one more concern. I asked Jenny to let Ryken know that I was sorry I had asked the doctors to reduce his sodium benzoate medication. I was afraid the medication was hurting him internally. I was so worried that the medicine was causing the diaper rash and the acidosis. "If the medicine caused you any pain, then I am truly sorry, Ryken. I was only concerned about your well-being and health."

Jenny relayed his message for me. "It did not matter. It did not—and would not have—changed anything."

Some of my guilt washed away. I was only trying to help my baby. It was helpful to hear Ryken's answer because guilt can be detrimental to the human spirit—and it was for mine.

Jenny said, "Ryken wants you to know that he is so sorry you are so sad. He never meant for you to be this sad after he died. He will always be with you, and he wants you to be happy."

I will never be truly happy ever again. How could I not be sad? Ryken is not here anymore. I was in such a state of anguish. I missed Ryken beyond words, but I was starting to understand that our departed loved ones only wish joy and happiness for us here. It was as though they did not understand our grief. On one hand, it was helpful to hear that Ryken wanted me to be happy, but I was in a place where it felt like an impossible challenge.

He had placed awareness in my realm of thought. *My baby wants me to find happiness again.*

My world had been turned upside down, and I was lost in a fog. Hearing my baby's pain at my own grief was a wake-up call. It was as though I had been woken up from a bad dream.

Your baby is still with you—with you always, in fact. You are only separated because you choose to think like that due to your grief. You choose to play with your ego instead of dancing with your higher self.

The ego is what separates us. When you remember how to connect to your higher self, then you can connect to me. That is where I am. I am there with the angels and your higher self. You can find me through talking with God. You can find me in the stillness of your mind when you meditate. Sitting quietly will allow us to connect. You only have to want to believe that I am still with you. I am still with you.

Ask the angels for help and they will show up to help you. You have free will, so you need to invite them into your life. By allowing them into your life, you will begin to heal with their subtle help. They will send you signs when you are ready. When you are open to seeking the answers, the answers will find you."

This is the new reality that I am trying hard to face.

Jenny shared with me that the next four or five years would be power years for me. She did not feel that I could be a full-time stay-at-home mom. I would need something else in my life. I listened to her words and guidance, but I had no words to convey back to her.

It was difficult to believe I would be having some power years when I was in a complete state of pain and sorrow. I was unsure about what the future held for me—or my family. I was still trying to process everything we had gone through with Ryken. I was a self-proclaimed control freak with no control of my life. I was flying by the seat of my pants and was desperately searching for any signs that were coming my way.

Jenny shared with me that in two weeks I would be coming out of the pain. I would begin to feel better. I hoped she was right. That seemed impossible, but I was open to feeling better. I was feeling wonderful at this moment in time. Maybe happiness was on the horizon for me. I was unaware of how to shift out of the emotional turmoil I was stuck in, but I was open to help from everyone, all sources, everywhere, on earth, and from the other side.

I was basking in the positive emotions that the session had instilled in me. Maybe there was hope again, but it would look different than I had imagined.

Jenny told me to hug Ryken every night before bed and tell him that I loved him.

Of course I can hug Ryken and tell him I love him every night. I already think about him and how much I love him a hundred times a day, so that won't be a problem.

I said, "Yes, I can do that."

The hard part for me is coming to terms that Ryken is with me always—just differently.

I said, "I want to come back and see you every week so I can talk to Ryken."

She looked me in the eye, with compassion, and said, "No. You can't come and see me every week, Pam. You will be able to feel Ryken at home. He is there with you. You can talk to Ryken there."

I was not convinced. I knew I would find a way to go back again and see her. She was a kind soul and could have said yes. In fact, she could have told me to come back every day to connect to him, and I would have.

I was desperately trapped in the muddy, murky waters of grief. I was beginning to drown, and I saw her as the lifesaver that would save me from my sorrow. I would do just about anything to connect with Ryken. It was nice that I was guided to a medium that had a strong value system in place. She did not take advantage of me in my time of need.

The session ended, and Ryken and Angel Sonya returned to the other side.

I miss him already, but I feel stronger. I feel like I can step forward with my life—at least for today. I know I can. It's a start. I know the troops are on their way to help me out.

I hugged Jenny for the priceless gift she had given me. The answers I received were beyond what I had imagined or hoped for. This experience was life changing for me.

The undeniable confirmation that Ryken was safe, happy, and cared for by an angel, mended pieces of my broken heart. Angel Sonya and Ryken found my cousin and were able to channel a message to her. The universe lined it up so I would receive Seraphina's message as validation that Ryken was with Angel Sonya. I knew the universe was trying to help me believe in something greater than the pain I was experiencing as a mother who had just lost her baby. The universe was working hard at helping me heal.

I had been given an angel carrying a toddler as a gift from the funeral. That angel meant more than anyone could realize. I christened her Angel Sonya in my mind. All I had to do was look at that figurine to make my heart start to mend. It would be a reminder.

My brain was still in overdrive. I was trying to make sense of it all. I took her card to share with my family. Maybe I would pass on her information to someone else. I was so full of admiration for this beautiful woman and her gift to connect to the other side.

I said a prayer to God and thanked him for sending me another earth angel to help me through my grief. I was still upset with him, but I felt as though he sent Jenny to help me as a peace offering. His olive branch might have worked because I was happy for the moment. I felt forgiveness flowing into my body.

I left the store and didn't even notice the cold. I was on cloud nine. On the drive home, I listened to "Fly" by Celine Dion, which we played at Ryken's funeral. I felt pure joy and love racing through me. On any other day, I would not have been able to listen to that song without having a full-blown anxiety attack. I knew Ryken was flying with his angel on the other side.

I felt giddy about all the information I had received. I thought about Ryken going to school and was curious about what he had learned from his journey on earth. Ryken was with angels and was learning about the past two months of his life. He was going to be in school soon.

That hour with Jenny had been nothing short of a miracle for me. Maybe it was the miracle that God had sent me. Maybe I was not completely ready to let go of my pain, but Ryken was still in my life. Maybe that was part of my life's purpose.

The questions were beginning to overwhelm me. I decided to let them go and leave them unanswered for the moment. I chose to take the gift of inner peace I had just been given and go with it for the time being. I was living in the present, and it felt good.

The most important revelation after my crossover session was realizing it was about Ryken's journey in this lifetime. It was going to help me climb out of my grief and depression and view my loss through a different lens.

Knowing I was part of his life lesson brought me a sense of peace and a deeper understanding about our destiny together. It helped me understand why we have all gone through and endured such pain. I left my visit with Jenny feeling a sense of peace and serenity.

I felt a sense of acceptance for the first time since Ryken was born. For the briefest of moments, I felt peace and contentment because talking with Ryken gave me a sense of serenity.

It was nice to hear that he was loved and cared for. He was a chatterbox and had quite a personality. I smiled at the description of my baby. My second son, my beautiful baby boy, Ryken.

The snow did not bother me at all. The weather was cold, windy, and miserable. Inside my car, I was warm and happy—elated even. I was going to ride the wings of joy for the moment. I was nobody's fool. I knew that grief would find me again, but I was free of it for the time being.

I arrived home and shared my news with Brett. I snuggled with Kaden in the rocker recliner. I asked Brett if the name Toby rang a bell for him.

Brett said, "Yes, I had a dog named Toby. I was five years old when we got him. He was my best friend. Why would you ask about Toby?"

He had never shared that information with me.

"Ryken asked Jenny to tell me that I was to say the word *Toby* to you."

Brett said, "Toby would walk my brother and me to and from school every day. He was my favorite dog."

I could tell how special that dog was to Brett. I knew why Ryken had asked me to share it with his dad. He wanted his dad to hear something that no one knew but Brett. How would Jenny and I know to say *Toby* unless Ryken told us from the other side?

Wow! Ryken was smart! He wanted to help his dad see through his skepticism and know that Ryken was okay. I hoped knowing that his beloved pet was with his baby on the other side would bring my husband some comfort. Maybe what I shared with Brett could help him believe in something greater than ourselves. It might give him something to ponder other than the reality of the pain and grief we were dealing with at this moment.

"Ryken does not like you chewing your nails. If he decides to come back, he wants you to stop that habit."

Brett looked at me and raised his eyebrows.

"I am only the messenger," I said. "You should listen to Ryken though."

It was quite interesting to be told something by your baby. I had been told many things and was still trying to make sense of it all.

I kissed Kaden and was so thankful that he was alive and healthy. He was there for me to care for and love—and he was free of NKH.

I was so excited about the reading that I called my mom and shared the news with her. I relayed Ryken's message to her and suggested a reading to talk to Ryken herself.

She agreed, and I offered to go with her. *It is the least I can do.* I'd always had a rebel in me, especially when I was fighting for a cause. There was no greater cause for me than my children. With Kaden and Ryken, there was nothing I would not do for them—no matter where they resided.

The days were going to drag until we were able to talk to Ryken again, but I would try to be patient. Maybe patience was one of my life lessons this go-around. I would have to think about it.

My aunt and uncle were visiting my mom and heard my story. Was it a coincidence? I think not. I asked them if they wanted Jenny's phone number to talk to Garret. I was unable to understand why they did not want to set their own crossover appointment to talk to him. They were both raised Catholic. I was the only teenager I knew who called her aunt and uncle and asked to go to church on Sundays. I really enjoyed going to church in my youth.

I still believed in God, but I was searching for something else. Whatever reason they had that prevented them from their own session with Garret was none of my business. *I am not here to judge.* They were kind enough not to judge me for having a crossover session.

We all have our own ways of dealing with our grief and loss. What resonates with one person may not resonate with another. I was learning that it was okay because we each had our own journey here to navigate through.

I am here to share the amazing gift I was given. If it helps someone decide they would benefit from a crossover reading to help deal with grief, then great. If they choose not to, then I respect their decision.

I know that I told God and the universe that I needed help. I was in search of someone to help me connect with Ryken. I needed answers immediately, and people showed up to help me and provide guidance and insight.

I would never pass up a chance to connect to Ryken. Thank you, God and Ryken, for leading me to Jenny! Angels, you astound me. I realize that I have you working hard over there, but I appreciate everything you do for me.

Every night, I have been reading books to my sunshine, Kaden, and tucking him into bed. I hug and kiss him and say, "I love you so much, Kaden."

He looks into my face and says, "Love you, Mom."

It is music to my ears.

He gives me the best hugs. This little boy needs me as much as I need him. I am intent on embracing my grief and healing for Kaden and for Ryken. Also for Brett and for myself. Our marriage and family deserves it.

I step into Ryken's room and turn his mobile on. I can feel him with me. My arms have goose bumps. I listen to the music and watch the teddy bears dancing. A smile forms on my lips, and I say, "I love you, Ryken."

I know he is here with me and that he says, "I love you too, Mommy."

I turn to leave and turn off his bedroom light. I go to bed and hug myself. I know my angel in heaven is with me. I look at Ryken's picture and the toddler with wings on my night stand. The figurine is a reminder of my chat with Ryken. I smile and say, "Good night, Kaden and Ryken. I love you both, my beautiful boys."

I kiss and hug Brett and thank him for being my husband.

"You're welcome. Thank you for being my wife."

I am overcome with gratitude that we are walking together in this journey called life. Sleep surrounds me, and I allow the night to take me away. My heart begins to heal, slow but sure, as my soul travels far and away.

My soul always returns by morning—just in time for my sunshine to wake up.

AFTERWORD

The fork in the road began for me on December 31, 2005. I chose to step forward and embrace the words and answers I was given by that beautiful earth angel. She was able to connect me with my beautiful baby on the other side. Through her gift, I was given the most priceless opportunity: a visit with Ryken.

I heard from my son's soul that he had his own journey to complete here. He had his own ship to sail, and he was the captain of his own destiny. I listened to his words about his life's purpose, which was when my own healing actually began. In doing so, I have found my life's purpose as well. I need to share his story—the one about his life on earth and the life he continues to live on the other side.

The gift of hearing how safe and wonderful he is doing over there has really catapulted me out of the sea of grief I was drowning in. He is not just in his coffin in the ground. That was the "physical form." That is where "his shell" he used to come to earth for his life lessons resides. The physical shell is no longer viable, and it was the vessel for Ryken when he was on earth: the beautiful body he was born into during this lifetime.

Ryken is in heaven with other babies and children like him. He is learning and processing what happened to him in his physical body on earth as the angels watch over him protectively. He is surrounded by love and light. He is full of peace and joy. Could I ask for a greater life for Ryken than that?

Yes, I could. I could ask that he be here living, full of life, with me on earth. Again that is about me—my own deep needs and my journey here on earth. That was not part of Ryken's journey. That was not the deal I made when I signed up to be Ryken's mom before I was born.

This is Ryken's journey. This is his life. I am a part of it, and I am learning from it. He has never really left me, and if I close my eyes, I can feel him. Even now, he is with me and cheering me on. He drops sentences in my head as I write this book, and my connection to him gets stronger every day. This is my miracle. This is what God had in store for me. I still have Ryken with me. It just looks different than I had hoped for or imagined. I am finding gratitude in having Ryken with me in this different way.

The last piece of knowledge I was given from my first crossover with him was that he never meant to hurt me and that he loves me very much. He is still around because of the pain I am feeling. I tell myself that I need to help myself resolve this pain. I am unable to help myself, and I do not know how to end my grief. Or does grief ever end? The longing I have for Ryken is affecting me on an emotional level. My grief is dark, and I need some light shed on me.

God says, "I have gifted you with the sun every day. Find the gratitude in that."

When Kaden walks in the room, my life is brighter. Yes I am grateful for my sun.

My higher self says, "Pam, you were smart enough to ensure you had a healthy firstborn to get you through Ryken's passing and to help you as you deal with your grief."

I hug Kaden and say, "You are my sunshine." I live in the moment and play cars to the best of my ability.

I am left with more questions. *Will we be able to have another baby? Was Ryken right?* In the grief world, when a family loses a baby, the next baby born healthy and alive is called a "rainbow baby." *Will we have a rainbow baby? Is a little girl waiting on the other side to become a part of our family? When will the geneticists know?* These questions have no answers right now. This is the lesson of patience that is hard for me.

Another lesson is learning to trust. I am focusing on my own intuition. I am allowing myself to trust as best as I can—considering what I have just been through. It is as though my soul is driving me toward the path I need to be on—even though I dig in my heels at times.

My plan of action right now is to release the inner pain, embrace the strength from the lesson, and allow the healing to begin. I watch for signs since I know I will be guided from the other side.

Another lesson for me is self-care. Whether I need help physically, mentally, emotionally, or spiritually, I am going to allow my own intuition to be my guide. I have asked for help, and I am willing to accept it when it is delivered to my doorstep. I am open to accepting help in any fashion. I know that God—with the help of my guides and angels—will send the right people and life circumstances to me when I need them.

When we take care of ourselves, the world blesses us with others who will help us on the next part of our journeys. Somehow. Some way. We don't understand why some things happen to us, but it will all make sense eventually.

Dear God, guides, and angels, I need help.

If we listen patiently, we are given guidance. It may look different than what we had hoped for. It may even be better than what we had imagined. The key is to release control and give it to God, spirit, our angels, and guides. It is having faith and trusting in something bigger than ourselves. This is another priceless lesson. It is difficult to do at times. If you think that's a load of crap, take comfort in knowing that I have thought that at times too.

Keep searching for answers that resonate within you. I searched until I found what my soul was looking for. If we are ready to go within and slay the ego by working through our grief, the victory is worth it.

A bright light goes off for the briefest of moments in my mind. *Ryken's life was about Ryken. I need to stop making it about myself and my loss. His life was not just about me. It was also about Ryken's journey on earth, and I was a big part of it.*

God, send me some help please—and thank you because I don't know how or what to do right now. I need some guidance and assistance, God. I am asking all the wonderful angels over there as well for assistance. Actually, I am begging for your assistance.

Ryken, my sweet baby, I am sure you are listening. If you can help as well, that would be great. Best of luck at school, my love, while you decompress. Angel Sonya, I know you can feel the gratitude from my heart because of the love and care you have for Ryken. Thank you from the very depth of my soul for putting what is left of my broken heart at ease for the moment.

A profound change in my thought process began. I had been strolling down Pity Lane for a while.

Poor me. I lost my baby.

Poor me. I don't have two little boys to raise.

Poor me, poor Brett. Poor Kaden has no baby brother anymore.

In order to take a detour, my thoughts had to take a turn. My first step was asking my guides and angels for help. I still needed help with my grief because I am only human. I needed someone to help me get through it and deal with the suffering. I asked God to send me someone who could help me. I knew I needed counseling. I needed someone who knew grief and who could help me understand about pregnancy and infant loss. I was experiencing a different grief than when I lost my grandmother and Garret.

There was a slow shift going on inside me. A seed was planted in my awareness, and it was starting to take root in my brain. It was going to grow slowly. I had been through the pits of hell, and I was trying to claw my way out.

I felt as though God had abandoned me when my pleas for a miracle went unanswered. The information that God was helping Ryken with his life's purpose helped wash away the superficial layer of pain I had been holding onto. There are still a lot of emotions at the core of my existence. There was no time to process any of them during the past few months. The word *miracle* triggers me very easily. I feel a surge of fiery red anger when I hear it. My *miracle* that Ryken would live did not happen. I still have a lot of self-healing to do. I am a self-proclaimed work in progress.

I am in dire need of support; sunshine and rain as well so I can continue to grow inside. I will need to nurture this seed of inner strength. It will grow big and tall someday. It will be strong and healthy, but there is work to do beforehand. My inner strength will thrive in the world for all to see someday—just not now. Like a turtle, I have to go within and take cover in my shell. I feel battered and bruised, and I know it is going to take a lot of time to heal.

My life is about having patience and trust. I'll take notes as I watch myself growing little by little. It will be worth it because something deep within is telling me so.

I am part of Ryken's journey, and this was his life. This is what he chose before he was born. This is what I chose before I was born. I choose to be his mom. My soul knew this was coming even if my heart did not.

My ego says, "Remind me to slap myself silly when I return to the other side for choosing this life path."

That is not even a joke; it is actually the truth. It is my truth.

My higher self says, "You and Ryken chose these experiences together so each of you could learn. You have helped Ryken. Now, you need to help yourself."

My ego is silenced for a moment. I have chosen not to play with it right now. Instead, I am dancing with my higher self. I am tuned in to a different frequency that will increase my vibration and leave me feeling more at peace with my life circumstances.

That was the moment my journey began to change directions with Brett and our sons. Kaden is here on earth, and Ryken is in heaven, but they are both learning what they need to.

Brett and I are learning what we need to as well. We stepped onto our new life paths, hand in hand, ready to begin the next step of our journey. *Will we find our baby girl at the end of the rainbow?* I am left wondering when we can begin *chasing rainbows* together in search of her.

ABOUT THE AUTHOR

Pamela Larocque is a woman who has many roles in her life. On a personal level she is a wife, mother, daughter, sister and friend. Professionally she is a Social Worker, an Energy Healer, an advocate of healthy living and an author.

Presently she is writing about her grief, her quest to find joy again after the loss of her second son, Ryken in infancy, from a rare genetic condition known as NKH, and living in the moment with gratitude to have a healthy child to love and parent. She plans to share this with the world in the sequel to Ryken's Journey which is called *"Chasing Rainbows"*.

She is also on her own journey to find herself again, the woman she was before her grief and the person she is now. Then somehow meld them together to be the person she is striving to become.

On a spiritual level, this book is part of Pam's life purpose and she has set out on a quest to fulfill her own soul contract in this lifetime. She is determined to learn her own life lessons and pass on the wisdom she has gained so others can heal as well. She believes that if we release the inner pain, embrace our strength from the lesson, then our healing will begin. In order to heal, it is important to embrace our life circumstances and acknowledge what we are feeling. When we walk through our grief with supports in place, we can find the pathways of love, joy and acceptance. This is how we can find our own inner light again and allow it to shine forth in the world while remembering ... *love is infinite.*

"Our Champion"

Though your stay was brief
you were a great teacher
and the lessons you taught
were profound
Just as memories of you
are all around
You have left footprints
on our hearts
Now only time remains
Until we meet in heaven
to hold you once again

Written by Ryken's Mom

love is

INFINITE...

Printed in the United States
By Bookmasters